D1531704

Life's NOTES

Down-to-Earth Insights for Well-Being

STEVE WARD

iUniverse LLC
Bloomington

LIFE'S NOTES
DOWN-TO-EARTH INSIGHTS FOR WELL-BEING

Medical Advice

The information, ideas, and suggestions in this book are not intended as a substitute for professional medical advice. Before following any suggestions contained in this book, you should consult your personal physician. Neither the author nor the publisher shall be liable or responsible for any loss or damage allegedly arising as a consequence of your use or application of any information or suggestions in this book.

Financial Advice

The information, ideas, and suggestions in this book are not intended to render professional advice. Before following any suggestions contained in this book, you should consult your personal accountant or other financial advisor. Neither the author nor the publisher shall be liable or responsible for any loss or damage allegedly arising as a consequence of your use or application of any information or suggestions in this book.

iUniverse books may be ordered through booksellers or by contacting:

iUniverse LLC
1663 Liberty Drive
Bloomington, IN 47403
www.iuniverse.com
1-800-Authors (1-800-288-4677)

Because of the dynamic nature of the Internet, any web addresses or links contained in this book may have changed since publication and may no longer be valid. The views expressed in this work are solely those of the author and do not necessarily reflect the views of the publisher, and the publisher hereby disclaims any responsibility for them.

Any people depicted in stock imagery provided by Thinkstock are models, and such images are being used for illustrative purposes only.
Certain stock imagery © Thinkstock

Library of Congress Control Number: 2013911434

ISBN: 978-1-4759-9556-5 (sc)
ISBN: 978-1-4759-9558-9 (hc)
ISBN: 978-1-4759-9557-2 (ebk)

Printed in the United States of America

iUniverse rev. date: 07/10/2013

Life's Notes: Down-to-Earth Insights for Well-Being is dedicated to our adult sons and daughter and our two young grandsons. The theme and message of *Life's Notes* is to help them and all of us live lives of abundant goodness in a challenging world. We all need reminders from time to time to follow the path of goodness to preserve our well-being. *Life's Notes* is a way to start questioning the paths we follow and evaluate their destination and their influence on our well-being. With this knowledge, we can add our own notes to complement *Life's Notes*.

"People always came to Steve with their troubles, as they could trust him. It seems natural that he wrote a book about well-being."—Deb Ward, special-education teacher for deaf/hard of hearing for thirty-five years

"Steve's previous book, *Finding Your Positives*, is not just another self-help book. It deserves to have a place on your bookshelf. I am pleased to recommend Steve's book to all who are struggling."—Linda Hewitt, confidence coach for twelve years

Contents

Acknowledgments

Writing the initial draft of a book is a solitary task requiring concentration and focus. Critiques and editing, as tough as they may be, are necessary to refine and polish the content for the enjoyment of the reader. Julie, my wife of thirty-eight years, brought the harshest critique, with my sister being a close second. They took the time to offer suggestions, always improving the message, and their blunt honesty was much appreciated.

Heartfelt gratitude also goes to our children and our daughter-in-law for their teachings, inspiration, and support. Also, thanks for putting up with my enthusiasm for this project that at times may have seemed overzealous.

Thanks to all who, over the decades, knowingly or unknowingly contributed ideas for topics and content as I listened to and observed them in daily life. Whatever situations or trials and tribulations we face, it's good to know that others—over time and with patience, motivation, and commitment—survived their ordeal to emerge a better person.

Thank you to all who cared for me at Barnes-Jewish St. Peters Hospital, where I recovered from my heart attack, and at the adjoining Siteman Cancer Center, where I received my cancer treatment. We should all share such devotion and compassion as caretakers in our community and family. I must express a warm thank-you to all on the Patient Family Advisory Council at Siteman Cancer Center and the Man-to-Man support group for their support and inspiration. Special thanks to fellow council member and author Chris Frey for his support to keep me writing.

A heartfelt thank-you to my dad, who passed away in 2000, and my mom, who passed away a few months ago, for all the fond memories, for their teaching by example the goodness of life, and for their passionate love of my sister and me. They will always be remembered dearly as God's blessing to the two of us.

Preface

*L*ife's *Notes: Down-to-Earth Insights for Well-Being* presents a powerful perspective into the elements of life that impact on our well-being, keeping us from a balanced, meaningful life. In sharing the wisdom and strategies I've gained from my experiences, I hope to enlighten your consciousness and guide you to grounded decisions when facing the intersections and crossroads of your own life.

After experiencing a diagnosis of cancer along with subsequent treatment, and then a year later suffering a heart attack requiring rehabilitation, I felt compelled to share insightful messages to motivate and inspire others suffering from life's challenges and obstacles. The combination of these two life-threatening challenges caused me to view life with a magnified perspective of awareness and consciousness to appreciate the good within and the good surrounding me. I believe that between the skills I've learned facing numerous challenges and my approach of "If it isn't something, it's something else," the book wrote itself. The theme of goodness for well-being was a natural one and flows through each of the notes.

Note 9, "Power of Gratitude," was the first one written. The power of gratitude for all the good in my life inspired a long list of potential notes. I drew upon other life experiences to continue to add to the list of notes to be shared. Notes 65 and 66 on positives as well as Note 6, "Heart Expansion," also inspired the addition of further related notes.

Intertwining relationships among the notes is part of the magic of exploring life's journey along a path of virtue. It is the harmonious influence of all notes playing together that fills life with meaning and purpose. This intricate network of notes will remind you to follow your path of goodness or inspire you to improve your life's journey and well-being, as it has inspired mine.

Introduction

Welcome to *Life's Notes*, a collection of ideas to promote well-being. Weaving your way through the book, you will learn the virtuous effects of numerous topics that can guide you to a balanced life of goodness. Life presents many challenges, obstacles, and temptations, jeopardizing your harmony and well-being. Each of the seventy-one notes included here introduces concise, easily digested information for easy reading and reference. Challenges, obstacles, and temptations periodically surface as we make our way through life, attempting to shift the balance of our well-being. The message of *Life's Notes* is both timely and timeless, providing meaningful help for today and hope for the future. The notes remind us to follow the path of goodness and be more aware of the importance of our well-being.

Parents of adolescents can use *Life's Notes* to teach the elements of goodness to their sons and daughters. New parents can consider it a book of short stories to share ideas with the little ones. Married couples and single adults will certainly be inspired by the powerful themes of *Life's Notes*. The common theme of goodness for well-being runs through notes addressing virtue, inspiration, curveballs of life, relationships, life skills, and other meaningful topics. Life is not always a bouquet of roses. Facing life's challenges is something we all confront with varying degrees of preparation and skill. The notes inspire thought and action to restore or sustain a healthy and balanced life.

As you read on, you will learn how all the notes intertwine and are dependent on each other to highlight a path of goodness. For sustainable well-being, follow the theme of goodness contained in *Life's Notes*. My goal is to get you to evaluate your well-being and think how you can improve yourself as a person. No matter your situation or environment, you have the capacity to improve and to inspire yourself and others.

Enjoy a thought-provoking tour through *Life's Notes*. After personal reflection on each note, write your thoughts on the pages at the end of each section to reflect on how you're doing dealing with challenges, obstacles, and situations. Use *Life's Notes* to incorporate or enhance the theme of goodness and well-being in your daily life. When you're having difficulty in life, it might be helpful to refer back to pertinent notes to remind yourself how to get back on track.

Become more disciplined and pay further attention to the role well-being plays in your life for meaning, purpose, and happiness. Periodically, or when suddenly facing a tough life challenge, do a check-up of your well-being to assess its condition, and see if you need to review some of the notes to restore meaning, purpose, and happiness. Like our cars, we too need tune-ups to address the pings and dings, run smoothly, and move forward.

PART 1

Well-being

Well-being is an often-misunderstood concept. The notes in this section look at our well-being in detail and explain why it's so important. You'll discover whether you have symptoms of a life that has fallen out of balance and find suggestions for restoring your well-being and living a life of harmony and balance.

Life's Note 1

Sustainable Well-Being

When is the last time you gave much thought to your well-being? If you're like most of us, you've ignored it, tried to mask any dissatisfaction you felt, and continued along with the status quo. Once you begin to realize the importance of your well-being and the impact it has on your ability to function effectively, you'll want to give it more attention.

> **Inspiration**
>
> *Your heart is your emotional gyroscope for balance and harmony.*

Well-being is associated with a good and positive life. We all have innate psychological needs to feel connected and accepted. A sense of belonging is integral to our well-being. Well-being indicates a perfect balance of all the facets of our being—psychological, emotional, social, physical, and spiritual. When all of these blend and work in synchronization, they permeate our life with happiness, calmness, peacefulness, purpose, and meaning. When they are out of tune, our well-being is severely compromised.

- *Psychological well-being* relates to a state of overall mental health marked by balance, harmony, and happiness. That doesn't mean we're completely free of challenging conditions or situations, just that we've learned to cope with them.
- *Emotional well-being* describes a state of pleasant feelings and thoughts. We can have emotional health even with manageable levels of anxiety and stress. Though we might hope to live a life completely free from confusing emotions, that's unlikely.
- *Social well-being* is a barometer of how well we do in social circles and relationships. Understanding the dynamics of social relationships including family, friends, and acquaintances is important for healthy, enduring relationships of mutual appreciation, respect, and happiness.
- *Physical well-being* seems self-explanatory, but in fact it's a state of good health not confined to our limitations or physical

challenges. We can have physical well-being at any shape, height, or weight. Contributing factors like diet, inactivity, and detrimental addictive habits do risk our physical well-being.

- *Spiritual well-being* indicates awareness of and gratitude for all the goodness surrounding us that feeds our mind, heart, and soul. Driving a life of spiritual goodness are faith, compassion, forgiveness, gratitude, acceptance, kindness, and hope. These are powerful forces to follow.

You'll know you have well-being when you experience a mind and life in order. Your mind has sound thoughts for grounded feelings and behaviors. A pleasant sense of satisfaction and calming peace permeates your mind, heart, and soul for days of meaning and purpose. You have an enlightened awareness that sustains your well-being for a higher quality of life.

Challenges occur throughout life, continually putting at risk our well-being and balance. Dealing with obstacles challenges our ability to maintain harmony, putting all facets of well-being in disarray. Do not be discouraged, as it takes patience and perseverance to maintain or restore well-being. Remain confident and do not give up.

If you find it difficult to sustain a state of well-being for extended periods of time, relax, as this is not unusual. Begin by taking small steps to focus on goodness and the positives in your life to protect your well-being. Achieving moments of goodness along the way paves the road to balance and harmony. Find time to rest at life's lookouts and review your inner landscape for a snapshot of your progress. Continue to build your album of life to appreciate your journey and your successes on your way to well-being.

Attitudes for Sustainable Well-Being

- healthy state of mind, heart, and soul
- striving for higher quality of life
- pleasant feelings
- positive emotions
- high self-esteem
- positivity of life

- enthusiasm
- happiness
- sound thoughts
- grounded behaviors
- feeling connected
- sense of belonging
- faith
- acceptance
- forgiveness
- compassion
- inner peace
- calmness
- appreciation
- gratitude
- hopefulness
- following goodness

Inspiration

Overall well-being resembles a symphony orchestra. All sections must play in harmony to enjoy life's music.

LIFE'S NOTE 2

Scale of Well-Being

The situations, circumstances, and challenges of your life can contribute to or upset your well-being. You should periodically check your emotional scale to see if your well-being is in balance or if the scale has been tipped. Just as you visit the doctor for physical checkups and the mechanic for diagnostics on your automobile, it's important to find time for personal emotional checkups to better take care of yourself and work to improve your daily balance.

When you feel off or out of sorts, take the time to evaluate your emotional balance. Feeling troubled, stressed, anxiety, anger, resentment, jealousy, guilt, or in a funk is a sign that it's time for a personal checkup. Develop the awareness to listen to your body, mind, heart, and soul. Your heart is your emotional gyroscope. Listen to your heart, and it will help you find well-being, balance, and harmony.

Some emotions may be in balance while others are far out of it, upsetting the scale of well-being. For example, all might be good in your life, but you feel stressed, and that has you out of balance and ruins your demeanor and your days. Stress, triggered by negative emotions, can be so strong it overwhelms you. Sometimes a number of emotions are slightly off-balance, and that collectively tips your scale in the wrong direction. Either way, your scale of well-being demands attention.

Harmony among our emotions is just as important as balance in bringing about well-being. Emotions can act alone or intertwine with others to tip well-being out of balance. Usually, if we feel stressed, it's because we feel anxiety, frustration, and possibly anger. Rarely is only one emotion out of balance. Knowing this, we can begin to see the urgency of checking our scale of well-being.

The following is an easy-to-use list that can help you measure your degree of well-being. Often we ignore our emotions and never even consider reviewing our emotional scale as often as we should. But our feelings not only affect our emotional balance but also our physical well-being. If you're starting to think you need to take your emotional temperature, you're probably already past the point at which you should be getting started.

Scale of Well-Being

How do you feel?

Balance	**Out of Balance**
Happy	Sad
Friendly	Lonely
Calm	Stressed
Accepting	Intolerant
Compassionate	Judgmental
Forgiving	Resentful
Grateful	Entitled
Peaceful	Angry
Content	Anxious
Comfortable	Overwhelmed
Trusting	Suspicious
Benevolent	Greedy
Kind	Inconsiderate

If the right column describes your feelings at any given time, do an evaluation to understand why and then take action to shift your emotional makeup to the column of balance on the left. Even if you only have one circled in the out-of-balance column, immediately give it attention to restore and maintain your well-being. Procrastination only exacerbates the situation, with additional emotions sliding out of balance, dragged down by the negative few. Early detection and action is the medicine for our feelings to be in harmony and our scale of well-being to be balanced.

LIFE'S NOTE 3

Table of Life: The Building Blocks for Well-Being

Chemistry has its Periodic Table of the Elements, a structured list to help us understand chemical properties. Yet we find limited charts of reference to explain the role of life's elements in our well-being. We invest little time and thought in improving our character to live lives of goodness with meaningful purpose.

Throughout our lives, we are bombarded by challenges or temptations that compromise our character and push us off the path of goodness. Like anything else in life, we need reminders of which elements truly matter to avoid the seductiveness of giving up and giving in to our shortcomings.

All the building blocks for well-being are related and intertwined, with each having equal significance and influence. Work to implement all of these elements into your daily life. It is possible to live a life of abundant goodness with all the elements of moral excellence. However, it is difficult and highly unlikely that you can follow all these elements each and every day. Life's beauty is derived from continually striving to do so. Stay the course to continue the journey of well-being.

Elements of Well-Being

- acceptance (approval as is, free of judgment)
- caring (feeling love or liking for the concern of others)
- compassion (deep empathy or sympathy, free of judgment)
- empathy (capacity to share in others' thoughts and feelings)
- enthusiasm (eagerness to share life's goodness with gusto)
- faith (belief, confidence, and trust to act responsibly)
- forgiveness (erasing the grudge of resentment and retaliation)
- grace (love, goodwill, and favor for others)
- gratitude (conscious awareness of the good within and around)
- heart expansion (love for self and selfless love for others)

- humility (placing others first, recognizing our shortcomings)
- inspiration (positive stimulation, influence, or motivation)
- kindness (sympathetic gentle courtesy)
- love (giddy feeling of affection, selflessness, passion, sacrifice, gifts)
- moral excellence (following the path of moral goodness)
- patience (calm endurance to persevere)
- prayer (consciousness of shortcomings, sharing and giving thanks)
- spirituality (nourish the soul for goodness and purpose)
- sympathy (compassion to share in others' emotions)
- tolerance (calm patience to accept others' views and habits)

Later, in Part 2, we'll look at some of these more closely.

LIFE'S NOTE 4

Wonders

Wonders of the World

Chichen Itza, Mexico
Christ Redeemer, Brazil
The Great Wall, China
Machu Picchu, Peru
Petra, Jordan (ancient city)
The Roman Coliseum, Italy
The Taj Mahal, India

Wonders of Humanity

Human cell
Birth of a baby
Human spirit
Our soul
Whispers of love
Warmth for animals
Forgiveness
Compassion
Gratitude
Inspiration

Think of the extent of influence and impact each item in either column has had on humanity and goodness. We face the choice of true beauty and wonder every day, whether it's external or emanating from within.

YOUR NOTES

How would you describe your current state of well-being?

How would you like to improve your well-being?

PART 2

Goodness

The components of goodness are many, and that can be a problem. Life offers conditions, situations, challenges, and temptations to distract us away from goodness. Our mind becomes consumed by how to deal with these circumstances, causing us to forget or find it difficult to recall the many components of goodness that could get us back on track. Notes in this section strike to the core of leading a life filled with goodness and purpose. Easy-to-follow bullet points will help you remember the elements of well-being and make goodness a habit.

LIFE'S NOTE 5

The Gift of Acceptance

I t is in our nature to question situations, occurrences, events, and challenges that occur throughout our lives. We have this inquisitive need to ask why and to think we can do better or change the outcome. Being overly inquisitive is our Achilles' heel, hindering our emotional growth by blocking our willingness to accept things that happen over which we have no control and people as they are in life.

> **Tip**
>
> Acceptance of self opens the heart for acceptance of others.

The concept of *acceptance* is misunderstood and sometimes misinterpreted as weakness, giving in, or giving up. This misconception hinders and complicates the process of self-awareness to practice acceptance free of judgment. Without acceptance, we live with the anchor of judgment and doubt always sinking us into the muck and mire of emotional dysfunction, keeping us from moving forward to improve ourselves and grow.

Recognizing situations and challenges that occur, acknowledging that they happened, and understanding that we cannot change what happened is the basis of acceptance. Initially, we may feel weak for having no control over events. Once we accept that, we begin to realize that from this point forward we can choose how we react and deal with all the ramifications.

Acceptance means having control of your emotions when hearing annoying news—like "Your appointment was rescheduled," "There could be side effects," "Treatment will take three months," as well as other nuisances—to remain rock solid through your journey to well-being. We usually have little control, if any, over what just happened. However, by accepting the situation and knowing we have alternatives, we can react constructively and minimize the damage to our confidence and demeanor. Acceptance puts us back in control with a positive attitude, heightened energy, motivation, strong will, and enthusiasm to make the best of a challenging situation.

We have an innate reluctance to simply accept who we are, and that slows our journey to self-awareness. Accepting yourself is the foundation of healthy self-esteem, belief in yourself, appreciating who you are, discovering your gifts, finding your passion, and loving yourself and others. We may see ourselves as less blessed with perceived external beauty than others, or less physically gifted, or with less perceived intelligence, or less talented. Forget these ridiculous comparisons, as they lead to self-doubt, self-pity, and low self-esteem, preventing you from discovering your true beauty.

The wrapping on a present is meaningless. It's the gift inside that has meaning. Look inside to find your gifts of meaning and purpose. They may be few or many, but the quantity is insignificant. Identifying your gifts along with their potential to create a better you is the reward of accepting who you are, as you are. You are a gift from God, a gift to family and friends, and a gift to yourself. You do make a difference.

Self-acceptance brings the confidence to be free of self-judgment and comparison, and from the influence of others' judgment, comparisons, comments, and criticism. This freedom presents time for thought and the ability to journey introspectively and discover and define yourself. You are now free from the past influence of allowing others to define you. Appreciate and give thanks for who you are. Celebrate your beauty just as you are.

Acceptance is not complete until we learn to accept others for who they are and appreciate the beauty of their gifts. Too often we try to change others for our own selfish judgmental reasons, when most likely we are the ones needing to change. When judging others, we miss opportunities to discover their inner beauty and gifts, which could make our world a better place. With others as with ourselves, acceptance is looking beyond the wrapping to discover the gift inside.

LIFE'S NOTE 6

Heart Expansion

Heart expansion follows a simple principle of physics: expansion and contraction. Materials and things in nature usually contract when cooled or frozen. The opposite effect is to warm or heat objects to make them expand. The amount something expands or contracts is called its *coefficient of thermal expansion*. We can follow this principle of physics to test the coefficient of thermal expansion of the human heart.

> **Quote**
>
> *Love is to open our heart to give meaning to our soul.*

Cooled and cold hearts are contracted, confining their capacity or freezing out the ability for connecting with all the good around and within. With a frozen heart, your daily personal weather resembles a blustery blizzard. You shiver inside, trying to survive days consumed by negativity and self-preservation from dawn until dusk. Trying to thaw a cold heart is like finding that one perfect snowflake on a mountain. Your frigid internal temperature and stormy personal weather is your extended forecast for freezing windchill, cooling your days and keeping you from discovering the healthy emotional benefits of heart expansion.

Thawing occurs when warm conditions are forecast on your personal weather map. Finding your positives, you kindle a fire within to warm your days, melt the negativity, and sweep away the drifts of detrimental emotions that have cooled your heart. Be patient; just as nature's thawing takes time, so does bringing warmth to your emotional weather forecast.

Magical things begin to happen when your cold heart starts to thaw and become warm. It gradually expands with the capacity to welcome goodness into your life. Heart expansion melts away negativity, pessimism, resentment, judgment, coldness, and impatience. You bask in the warmth of acceptance, love, compassion, forgiveness, tolerance, patience, and happiness.

Follow the practice of goodness to discover and enjoy the dynamic principle of heart expansion. We all have the capacity for a warm heart.

All we need is the inspiration to recognize and share life's abundant goodness. To sustain a warm heart, focus on positives and goodness; continue pumping goodness to continually expand your heart. No matter the weather outside, establish a habit of heart expansion to benefit from your personal weather forecast of soothing, warm tropical days. Yes, your heart can be warmed. Give in to your capacity for goodness and well-being. Search deep inside your being to find your positives, the things that truly matter in life; they will feed your heart and soul. Begin by finding one positive and use it to expand your heart, making it easier to discover more positives until you have a pile of them to draw upon when your heart needs some tender kindling.

Heart expansion brings awareness of all that is good in our lives, so that we can express appreciation and gratitude—sharing with people who are close, important, or influential in our lives what they truly mean to us and saying thank you. Practicing heart expansion, you will learn to unselfishly open your heart to welcome others into your life, to touch their heart and let them touch yours. The risk of heart expansion is the vulnerability for our heart to be bruised. Yet, surprisingly, the warm openness of heart expansion heals a bruised heart quicker than a cold one. Heart expansion offers minimal risk with maximum reward.

A warm heart is an open heart, full of acceptance, enlightenment, compassion, forgiveness, and goodness, with an unlimited capacity for family, friendship, and love. Heart expansion is the gift to accept and welcome others.

LIFE'S NOTE 7

Footsteps to Humility

Humility—selfless giving to help others while expecting nothing in return—is a never-ending test of our commitment and character. Without reminders and examples, it becomes easy to stray from living a life of humility. When we make it our motto to expect nothing in return, we remain humble. Following the path of humility requires the courage to stand with others, looking eye to eye rather than looking down. With humility comes the wisdom to see the best in others instead of what we can get out of them. Thinking we are humble is a hollow exercise; it is only in practicing humility that we share this spiritual gift.

> **Quote**
>
> *Serving others expecting nothing in return is walking the path of humility.*

Humility is the ability to recognize where we fall short. It encourages us to better ourselves and contribute to the betterment of others. Devotion to humility involves choosing acceptance over intolerance, compassion over judgment, praise over criticism, and community over self. Once you embrace humility, there is no boastfulness or thinking of yourself before others. Building bridges is the craft of humility. Humility is a gift to be shared for the betterment of all. If you expect something in return, humility is lost.

Too often, humility is misinterpreted as weakness, but the opposite is true. A life of humility requires strength of devotion and faith. It is this strength that shares respect for all beings, free of doubt and rank. Empathy forms the cornerstone and compassion the pillars of humility. Follow these virtues to walk with others, sharing the grace of belonging.

We have a natural need to feel appreciated. Belonging gives our soul meaning and purpose. Spirituality teaches us that there is more to life than mere existence. Another lesson of humility is gratitude to appreciate the goodness within and around us. These are additional forces to help us discover, test, and teach divine faith to live a humble life.

What we have within is a burning desire to search deeper for the true meaning of life. Our thoughts migrate from materialism to simplicity and spiritual clarity. Our soul, heart, and mind work as one as we think more often of others and less often of ourselves.

Footsteps of Humility

- compassion
- empathy
- acceptance
- grace
- spirituality
- faith
- gratitude
- simplicity
- belonging
- equality
- community

LIFE'S NOTE 8

Compassion or Judgment

Too often, we tend to pass judgment on others without considering compassion. We may not approve of people's appearance or mannerisms. We reject them without knowing their story; we decide to be the jury. Who are we to pass judgment? We haven't walked in their shoes—and even if we have, everybody's circumstances, environment, emotions, and ability to cope with life's challenges are different. How did we decide to anoint ourselves as the authority to pass judgment on anybody? Judgment robs us of the opportunity to learn and grow as a friend and be a better person.

> **Quote**
>
> *Compassion is softening someone's pain; judgment is missing the opportunity.*

Rather than judge, embrace the opportunity to reach out and help. By offering assistance, you benefit yourself as much the person you help. Compassion removes the cloud of judgment, opening your heart to empathy, understanding, and acceptance for the struggle of others. Compassion means listening with heartfelt support during someone's emotional time. When a person is dealing with their struggle alone, walking a dark and narrow path with an overgrown canopy shading the warmth of the sun, their prescription for encouragement is to have a friend to walk hand in hand with them and be their sunshine of compassion for a path of brighter, more abundant days. Be that friend.

When people are struggling, they find it hard to take the first step to ask for help; they are usually too embarrassed to be seen as weak. When you step forward to offer help, you soften their embarrassment and allow them to let someone into their circle of emotional chaos. Bring friendship and warmth to encourage hope. You will be the inspiration for building steps from the abyss of despair to the solid footing of well-being and balance.

Compassion can be as simple as empathizing or sympathizing with someone facing a problem or a difficult situation, trying to help someone solve a problem, or sharing ideas to ease a difficult situation. Acceptance is another form of compassion. Accept people as they are and who they are, free of judgment.

Compassion or judgment—that is your choice. Choose wisely, using the scale of goodness, and compassion will rule. Opportunities to step forward and grow come around only so often. Seize the opportunity. Think with your heart to grow and be free from judging. Thinking solely with your brain fosters short-circuited thoughts that cloud your ability to make good decisions. Your heart feeds your brain and nourishes your soul. Prepare a plate for an open warm heart and avoid a diet of judgment from a thick skull and a hardened heart. Choose the heart-healthy food of compassion to enlighten your being with goodness. Daily servings of compassion feed your well-being and help you to achieve and preserve harmony and balance in your life.

A heart of compassion or a heart of judgment, a warm heart or a hardened heart—choose carefully, as the decision makes the difference between serenity and warmth or a confusing coldness of heart. Following the rule of compassion brings opportunities to contribute for abundant, bountiful meaning and purpose in your life.

LIFE'S NOTE 9

Power of Gratitude

Expressing gratitude—thankfulness—is a choice. We have the choice to be grateful or simply ignore gratitude and its positive effects on our health and well-being. Gratitude is consciousness and awareness of all the good within and surrounding us. Welcome gratitude into your life to experience a warm transformation to appreciation and happiness.

Gratitude means understanding and acknowledging the simple kindnesses of life and the deeply rooted aspects within that define our goodness and spirit, benefiting ourselves and others. Include thankfulness for the simple pleasures of life—freshly baked cookies, sunny days, the scale showing you lost a pound. Deeply rooted goodness is the stuff that truly matters, such as forgiveness, compassion, tenderness, and love. Giving thanks for simple things and acts of kindness leads to a daily habit of gratitude. No matter the depth of the gratitude you express, its cumulative effect will be profound on your quality of life.

For gratitude to develop, you must consciously be aware of everything around you. Accepting things just as they are, free of interpretation or critique, is the basis for a methodology that finds the will to give thanks for all the good in good situations and the good in challenging situations. Once you have mastered the ability to find the good in bad situations, you have started to discover the power and peace of gratitude.

Your mind and heart are now free and open to perceive the good in all things. With this fresh perspective, you see things differently through the lens of acceptance and appreciation. Humility draws you to a state of consciousness in which you can enjoy positivity free of the limits of judgment. Your spirit, eyes, heart, and mind are all open to experience happiness and enjoy a fulfilling life of meaning and purpose.

Start sowing the seeds of gratitude to cultivate your imagination, dreams, and soul. Be kind to others, inspiring them to give thanks. Greet someone each day and say thank you to spread the power of gratitude. Gratitude for self and life is the catalyst to expressing kindness.

Developing a daily habit of gratitude requires practice and record-keeping. Begin today to practice gratitude with this simple process: Every day, write down three simple things you choose to express thanks for. Continue this process for one week with no repetition of previous mentions. At the end of the week, you'll have twenty-one examples of gratitude. The second week, continue writing three simple pleasures each day to give thanks for and add one deeply rooted aspect within for which you are grateful. After two weeks, you'll have forty-two simple mentions of kindness and seven deep, heartfelt expressions of gratitude. Each day, add one simple kindness or recognition of something to express thanks for. Periodically review your gratitude list of previous mentions or add new inner kindnesses or goodness to give thanks for. A journal, calendar, or daily notes in a jar seems to work best as a reminder of the power gratitude has on your life. The recording and reviewing of gratitude nourishes the practice of gratitude and helps it flourish as a habit.

Perspectives on Gratitude

- Grateful people seem to have greater appreciation, optimism, happiness, enthusiasm, and energy.
- Those embracing gratitude seem to have healthier and happier relationships.
- Gratitude has the capacity to lead people away from judgment to the healthier path of compassion and empathy.
- Life has taught me that spirituality seems to play an important part in teaching goodness, with prayer teaching us gratitude.
- Gratitude seems to assist with emotional balance.
- Gratitude teaches us to expand our heart for a greater capacity for love.
- Life's personal experiences and observations indicate that gratitude contributes to our well-being, filling us with meaning and purpose.

Discover the power of gratitude.

LIFE'S NOTE 10

Grace of Forgiveness

Forgiveness continues to be difficult for us to express and also to understand the significance of. Maybe it's because we are not sure why we should forgive, or do not know how to forgive, or have never forgiven. A hardened heart may not have the capacity or the willingness to forgive. No matter our limitations, forgiveness brings grace to heal and help us move on for our own well-being.

Many events in life—from the trivial breaking of a material possession to the harm of a loved one and all in between—are situations for forgiving. We may consider forgiveness, but our emotions keep us from understanding the how and why.

Emotional forgiveness is the most challenging. Our emotions range from sadness, hurt, and bitterness to betrayal and revenge. Since forgiveness does not come easy for most of us, time drags on and on before we decide to consider forgiveness. During this time of confusion, we hold a grudge and can't even begin to approach the point of considering forgiveness. Instead, we continue to float aimlessly in a twilight zone of conflicting and distorted emotions, delaying us from acting with the grace of forgiveness.

Your heart is your gyroscope for navigating through the labyrinth of detours, twists, and turns directing you away from forgiveness. Listen to your heart and let it guide you through this emotional maze. Trust your heart to provide the compassion, wisdom, and love to best serve you as the healing process begins. Be patient as your heart gradually directs you to the desired destination of forgiveness. Clarity will slowly emerge with calm and peace for the serenity and grace to forgive.

Faith gives us a foundation to understand right from wrong and good from bad. Do you continue to follow the path of sadness, bitterness, betrayal, hatred, and revenge, or do you follow the healing power of forgiveness? Have faith and walk the path of forgiveness. You will emerge a stronger person.

With faith and a warm heart willing to forgive, the act of forgiveness becomes a conscious choice of goodness. Transforming to a forgiving state of consciousness is a journey through haunting heartache and destructive emotions to appreciate the gift of forgiveness as well as the lessons learned from forgiving. You can now move forward and live with gratitude for all the good surrounding you.

How do you forgive? Simply look others in the eye, put a hand on their shoulder or shake their hand or give them a hug, and speak words of forgiveness. The most important thing is to be serious with meaning and good intent. Your heart will tell you when the time has come to forgive. Procrastinating will kindle the flames of difference dividing people from the goodness of a healthy relationship. Find the courage to forgive to save yourself and your relationships.

What Keeps Us from Forgiveness

- severity of the act
- hardened heart
- don't know where to begin
- don't know how
- don't know what to say
- fear
- rejection

Quote

Forgiveness comes from the heart. Freedom comes from forgiving.

Why to Forgive

- healing
- ability to move on
- peace
- well-being
- freedom
- live again
- new awareness
- gratitude

LIFE'S NOTE 11

A Whisper of Love Echoes Loudly

Why is it so many of us are hesitant to say "I love you"? When we are in the midst of a relationship, speaking words with such a powerful message carries the risk of harming or ending the relationship before it can blossom into a beautiful flower. In dating or the older version of courtship, vulnerability and the risk of commitment can make us reluctant to say "I love you." When these magical words are spoken out of obligation or with insincerity, the other may read the emptiness in them. Those three words, "I love you," are not to be taken lightly. If we again speak them with insincerity, can anyone believe what we say is what we mean, or is there only emptiness?

"I love you" is not to be spoken by the fainthearted. Love is unselfish, existing for the goodness of the one we love above our personal needs. The words "I love you" are so powerful that they can warm hearts, mend hearts, and bond hearts. Not saying "I love you" can break hearts.

A whisper of love echoes loudly. When you say "I love you" with heartfelt affection, the words resonate in the one touched to ensure that he or she has a wonderful day. When spoken without feeling and conviction, however, the words have no meaningful reverberating echo. Saying "I love you" from the heart ignites emotions deeply, with the message that the other is important and means so much to us that we need that person in our life. Needing people we love is the foundation that feeds us with meaning and purpose for a fulfilling life of connection, affection, commitment, and love.

Hearing we are loved sends tingling, rolling waves of feeling we are appreciated and touches our heart so deeply that we want to share experiences and create fond memories. Being loved hugs us with tender affection of comfort, contentment, and happiness.

How to love? There is one answer and only one answer, and that is complete love. Often we hear the term *unconditional love*. This implies the existence of conditional love, expecting something in return. But there is no such thing as conditional love. If there are conditions (limitations), is it love? If the words, "I'll love you if . . ." or "I won't love you if" . . . or "If you love me . . ." are spoken, conditions have been set. Conditions create obstacles, preventing or erasing true love. The word for this would be *like*. We can like someone dearly without loving them. Some examples of this might be a friend, a fellow student or coworker, or a neighbor. However, it is possible to love in these relationships as well.

We can love people in different ways. We love our spouse differently from a relative, children differently from a friend, and pets differently from people. This does not mean we love less or love more. We love differently.

Love begins with family. From the beginning, we are blessed with feelings of love. A mother holds her baby close; a father cradles his child to comfort the little one and see that magical smile only a baby can give. Love begins early and should endure through thick and thin, good and bad, and all of life's tough challenges. Love gives us the resiliency to survive and emerge a better person from all that is thrown our way throughout life. Should we love less if those we love become ill, permanently injured, have a scar, lose a job, or need help? With true love, the bond runs deep and stays the course no matter what. Love is acceptance, patience, and commitment. It is not a hobby.

Whispers of Love

- I love you.
- I miss you.
- I can't wait to see you.
- You mean everything to me.
- You are cuter than ever.
- I'm so glad you're my spouse.
- You look awesome.
- Thanks for being you.
- You are the best.
- We make a great team.
- You are perfect.

Pillars of Love

- emotion
- compassion
- commitment
- compromise
- communication
- forgiveness
- inspiration
- golden moments of celebration
- enthusiasm
- respect
- acceptance
- teamwork
- affection
- saying "I love you"

LIFE'S NOTE 12

Make Kindness a Habit

K indness encompasses so much that is good and gracious in our lives to help us seek emotional, spiritual, and physical health. To better understand kindness, consider a closer look at the combined dictionary meaning of *kind* and *kindness*: essential character, sympathetic, gentle, benevolent, gracious manner, pleasant, and favorable. To summarize, kindness is an essential habit for favorable, gracious pleasantry.

> **Quote**
>
> *Kindness is like a river; it starts small, and gains momentum to flow freely.*

Characteristics of Kindness

Care	Closeness	Compassion	Consideration
Courtesy	Favor	Fondness	Generosity
Gentleness	Good deed	Goodness	Graciousness
Heart	Helpfulness	Kindheartedness	Mindfulness
Patience	Softheartedness	Sweetness	Tenderness
Thoughtfulness	Tolerance	Understanding	Unselfishness

Practice the art of kindness to spread its goodness and help others discover its significance and importance in daily life. Kindness is truly an art, with a palette of warm, inspiring hues to add color to our days. Your heart is the brush and your soul is the inspiration. Paint often with imagination to make kindness a habit.

Kind thoughts, kind feelings, kind attitude, and kind demeanor are all well and good, but without action, there is no kindness. Nourishing the heart and soul with inspiring, warm emotions for personal and spiritual growth requires us to take the initiative to act. Kindness only happens when kind acts feed the spirit with beneficial, healthy positive emotions. Opportunities abound for acts of kindness:

- Plan a surprise date night with your partner.
- Have dinner with your son or daughter.
- Schedule a family fun activity.
- Tell friends and family how much you appreciate them.
- Call parents or children to tell them you love them.
- Leave kind notes for those you love and appreciate.
- Accept others just as they are.
- Give someone flowers for no special reason.
- Cook someone's favorite meal.
- Bake cookies to give to others and groups.
- Run an errand for someone.
- Take a caregiver to a movie or lunch.
- Sit with someone to give a caregiver a break.
- Compliment people.
- Share hugs and smiles.
- Listen to others with genuine interest.
- Give a tender pat on the shoulder or back.
- Greet people warmly.
- Cook dinner to surprise someone.
- Do someone else's tasks around the house.
- Hold the door open for someone.
- Address people by name.
- Inspire someone with touching words and tender action.
- Give someone a present for no reason.
- Bake a cake to give away.
- Give blood.
- Volunteer at a hospice or homeless shelter.
- Just volunteer.
- Drive others to appointments.
- Visit the elderly or a shut-in.
- Help others with projects around their place.
- Let someone go ahead in line at the grocery store.
- Wave a fellow driver to merge into your lane.
- Pay for someone's drink at a convenience store.
- Thank someone in uniform.
- Try saying yes instead of a quick no.

Create a custom list for acts of kindness, including the three Ws: who, what, and when. These three Ws establish a plan to take action to spread kindness. As time passes, add to your list with fun and creative ideas to show your appreciation for others.

LIFE'S NOTE 13

Awaken Spirituality

S pirituality is an inherited quality of consciousness that drives us to search for our sense of being and an enduring sense of purpose and meaning. Spirituality provides us with the principle of wholeness. Spirituality directs us along a path of core values based on morality throughout our journey of life. We have the choice to awaken our spirituality or continue to ignore it and allow it to hibernate. A second natural trait common to all is our soul. Our soul has the power to awaken the dynamic force of spirituality.

> **Quote**
>
> *Spirituality awakens goodness, giving meaning to life.*

The common dictionary meaning defines spirituality as of the spirit or the soul, being sacred, being religious, and dedication to God or spiritual things or values over material or temporal ones. The concept of spirituality can be seen as complicated when instead it is quite simple. Spirituality nourishes the soul for a life filled with goodness, meaning, and purpose.

Some would say that spirituality is religious. Indeed, religion is spiritual. Does this mean that those who do not attend a church, synagogue, or mosque cannot be spiritual? Of course not, as there are paths of nature, philosophy, mysticism, and the arts to find spirituality.

This is not to diminish the influence of religion on spirituality. Religion offers repetition, consistency, faith, belief, and stability to foster a place of peace and meditation for learning and sharing the teachings of God. Attending church on a regular basis builds the foundation of faith to believe that there is much more. We walk with spiritual footsteps to appreciate and celebrate all that has been created and ascend to the peace of everlasting life.

Spirituality is a relationship with a moral and value-oriented belief system and/or a relationship with God. Either way, spirituality is an individual and personal relationship based on intimate communication. Meditation is a form of spiritual communication. Praying is another example of intimate communication. Prayer is quiet time alone to express thoughtful whispers, thoughts spoken out loud, or written expressions of thanks, forgiveness, and more. Expressing your mind, heart, and soul with honesty cleanses the body of misgivings and wrongs. Prayer feeds and preserves spirituality and our soul.

Some may say that a divine being is the basis of spirituality and attending church is the foundation. We are not qualified to judge the spirituality of those who do not attend church but do live a life filled with compassion, kindness, forgiveness, goodness, and love. Society has the tendency to rush to judgment before considering compassion. Thinking we can pass judgment tarnishes and puts into question our own spirituality.

Being spiritual focuses more on compassion and guides us to strive to eliminate judgment. Spirituality gives us the patience to slow down and think with our heart before reacting with negative judgmental behavior. In addition, spirituality teaches us to follow the characteristics of goodness. We all have the opportunity and ability to choose the gift of spirituality.

Spirituality magnifies our goodness within, our core values and morality, and our faith and belief system to make the most of our finite time here on earth. With grounded spirituality, our heart is warmer with appreciation and acceptance of all the good within and surrounding us. Within our soul, we have a heightened awareness of the peace and purpose to express gratitude for each and every day. We trust that tomorrow will support, encourage, and maintain our path of spirituality.

If you question or doubt the power of spirituality or a divine being, take a moment to look to nature, the sky, and beyond. Look at the wonder of pictures taken by spacecraft and telescopes that show the vastness of space and the grandeur of earth. The beauty of all this did not just happen from a single atom. All this beauty and wonderment was either created by or encouraged and accelerated by the intervention of a divine being, God. Give thanks for God's goodness.

LIFE'S NOTE 14

Soften Your Thoughts and Words

The human body has no sharp edges. We are covered with soft to medium-soft, pliable, protective, and healing skin. Under our skin is God's version of memory foam to help keep our form. The exterior of our body is extremely resilient.

Looking to the interior of the body, we continue to find no sharp edges. Even our heart and mind are free of sharp edges. We are a geometric miracle with lines free of sharp corners. So if we are so smooth, why is it we sometimes revert to thinking and speaking words with sharp cutting edges hurtful to others?

> **Tip**
>
> *Think with the heart; speak from the soul to connect with love and compassion.*

Speaking with intent to hurt or embarrass others is a character flaw flowing with sarcasm, criticism, belittling, peer pressure, bullying, and name-calling. Words honed with sharp cutting edges hurt others more than we realize. Does the pain lessen if we do this subconsciously? The person on the receiving end will tell us no. Inflicting pain like this strains and even destroys friendships and family relationships. So why do we do this?

Often, this behavior stems from a need for power, supremacy, or control—or from self-doubt, poor self-esteem, or other conflicting emotions. No matter the cause, abusive words are hurtful and sometimes cause irreparable harm in relationships. Behavior like this is usually directed at people with limited opportunities to escape this damaging abuse. The victims are most often family members and children, who are scarred by this undeserved and unwarranted verbal abuse. Imagine the fear they must feel, as well as the loss of feeling loved and the degradation of their self-esteem and self-worth. Verbal abuse leads to overwhelming stress, causing both emotional and physical issues immediately or later in life requiring professional attention.

When we listen to someone speak with sharp edges and laugh, we condone this behavior and are as responsible as the one speaking the abusive words. Avoid the trap of condoning such behavior and its burning negativity. Step in to come to the support of the person being verbally abused. Strong people face the fear of reprisal and stand tall to say "no more" and support their loved one or friend. The weak stand idly by or join in the delivery of the sharp words. We have a responsibility to get involved for the safety of those being verbally abused. Imagine the future of their life if we continue to stand by and do nothing. Step forward to help the victims of verbal abuse.

Think of the other person's feelings before speaking and the impact of your words. Think not only with your mind but with your heart as well, and choose words free of slashing edges. Encouraging and supporting others with goodness is far more rewarding and lasting than a brief moment of hollow satisfaction.

No one deserves to be the victim of abusive thoughts and words. Life is a gift unlike any other. Live yours responsibly to grow within, sharing your warm gifts to nurture the spirit and lives of others, while at the same time nurturing your own well-being.

As difficult as it may seem, we also need to have compassion for those delivering this abuse. Usually there is some deep-rooted reason for uncontrollably acting with such abusive behavior. Judgment, as in most situations, is a disservice to all involved. Find it in your heart to feel empathy for how they must be hurting inside. They are embarrassed or unsure of what to do to become a better person. They may be acting wickedly, but inside there is warmth in their heart begging to be awakened. The conflict is, they are unsure how to awaken their heart and soul to correct this hurtful behavior and walk a path of goodness.

We can lead by example and be the catalyst to enlighten these verbal abusers to awaken their potential to be a better person. Professional help is another option for assisting those who use hurtful words to restore relationships and have a brighter future. No matter how this behavior is addressed, we must get involved to protect the victims of verbal abuse, and find goodness to soften our own thoughts and words.

LIFE'S NOTE 15

Scale of Beauty

For decades, men and women have been mesmerized by physical beauty. We spend billions of dollars annually to enhance our appearance. Every year there are countless beauty pageants awarding the most beautiful with a crown, flowers, and gifts. Our obsession with physical appearance demands there is a runner-up to step in if the winner is unable to continue. We don't find it necessary to have a runner-up in the World Series or the Super Bowl in case the winner is unable to continue. This need for a runner-up in a beauty contest illustrates both our being enamored with physical beauty as well as our personal insecurity with appearance.

> **Inspiration**
>
> The eyes see the picture.
> The heart discovers the beauty.
> The soul appreciates the story.

Industries have been built to physically alter or reconstruct our physical appearance because of our vanity. We feel inferior or are driven to become someone different. Acceptance of self and others as we are and for who we are seems to be a fading virtuous quality. However, there are times when reconstructive surgery is a blessing for those people suffering from a tragedy scarring their appearance. It is times like this when reconstructive surgery is a blessing to restore a person's outward appearance and reawaken inner beauty.

Society seems to endorse and be comfortable judging a person's appearance. Men and women both use the beauty scale of one to ten, with ten being beautiful and one being at the opposite end of our personal perceived scale of appearance. This practice continues today, and why? Imagine a girl or young woman walking by a group of boys or men holding court of judgment, and she hears she is a three or four or less. Testosterone-driven self-centeredness or verbal bullying—maybe they are one and the same. Think of the impact this practice can have on a person's confidence, self-esteem, and relationships. This type of narrow-minded bullying needs to stop.

In the art world—specifically painting, drawing, and sculpture—it is said that beauty is in the eye of the beholder. The art world is more gracious with its interpretation of beauty than we are. Art is seen as more than what appears on the canvas or a lump of clay formed into a shape. Each piece of art tells a story. The interpretation of the story is subjective.

We would be better served if we viewed people as works of art. Each of us is a piece of art to be appreciated. Our appearance is the painting of our window to our story. Accept others' appearance for the opportunity to hear their story and possibly be inspired to become a better person, filled with acceptance and compassion.

Perceived physical beauty does not correlate with happiness or healthy self-esteem. Accepting others, no matter their appearance, could be a gift that allows those people to trust us to be comfortable as they express their personal struggles and hope in some way we can help them. This is when inner beauty can surface.

Rather than be judgmental of others' appearance, focus on what's inside to see their beauty. A farmer or someone who works outside all day might have a weathered appearance, with rough skin and premature wrinkles. Try to imagine his story to appreciate his beauty. Open your eyes to see the beauty and the touching story of those who are physically impaired or impoverished. Judging on a scale of one to ten clouds our vision and cools our heart to a full appreciation and experience of the beauty surrounding us. Clear your blurry vision and expand your heart to discover the beauty of each face and open the window to the story waiting inside.

Beauty is not a contest. Appreciate the painting to see the beauty of the story.

LIFE'S NOTE 16

Discover Generosity

nside each of us is an opportunity indifferent to our position and lot in life. All are welcome to experience and share in the virtue of generosity. This is a door, and we should want to enthusiastically cross its threshold to feel its goodness and kindness. Once inside, generosity is at our fingertips. We need only open our hands and heart to welcome generosity into our life.

We may have reservations before deciding to pass through the door of generosity. Too often, generosity is associated with the charitable giving of money. Not all of us have the financial comfort or wherewithal to share monetarily. Passing through the door, we discover that generosity is much more than monetary donations. Generosity is a willingness to freely share ourselves and our gifts. Seeing what is behind the door awakens our consciousness to invite generosity into our life and discover its grace.

Generosity begins with us. The strength of being generous seems to be felt more deeply and appreciated more when we act before being asked. Our initiative and expecting nothing in return are the grace of generosity. Being generous knows no bounds.

There are so many additional ways to express generosity other than the customary donations of money for charities to do their work. Selfless giving of our being allows us to share our gifts and let generosity flow every day. Each of us has the potential to share our core of goodness in multiple ways to benefit those struggling and less fortunate.

Ideas of generosity remain idle thoughts until we act on them. To encourage yourself to take action, establish gratitude as a foundation of your being. With gratitude, open your eyes, mind, and heart for greater awareness of the opportunities and situations in which to be grateful. Express both gratitude and generosity from your heart.

Eagerly encouraging others might seem a simple act of generosity. However, for the person encouraged, it could mean a life-altering step to improvement. For some of us, our ego or self-centeredness gets in the way, prompting us to criticize others before considering encouragement. Consideration for others requires generosity from within. Encouragement and consideration are two stepping stones to expanding our generosity.

Sensitivity for others' feelings and thoughts remains a difficult task for some of us. Being sensitive to others is a generous consideration we can practice to become a daily habit. Sensitivity, especially among men and to a lesser extent among women, is often perceived as weakness, when in reality it shows strength of character. Sensitivity contributes to our strong core of goodness, our endearing personality, and our generous spirit.

For those of us who share the art of awareness of our surroundings and the light of others, kindness is a fruit tree bearing acts of goodness to touch the hearts of those around us. Kindness begins by recognizing opportunities and situations open to encouraging and healing acts. Somebody might be down and out, hurting, lonely, or in need of help, presenting opportunities for kindness that many of us miss or choose to ignore. With situations like this, say yes to generosity and offer help. Once you say yes, seize the opportunity to act. It does not matter who receives more from a kind gesture. But do know this, that both the one receiving and the one giving are made better by this generous act.

The two powerful core acts of generosity, empathy and compassion, are both easier said than done. Too often we are so caught up with work or our personal affairs that we shelter ourselves from sharing in the feelings of others. We might hear them reaching out for a receptive ear but choose not to listen and move the conversation in another direction or cut it short to ignore their feelings. Instead, listen with your heart and offer empathy and presence to help them with their struggle. Compassion is certainly an act of kindness that is initiated in your heart and endures with practice. Both compassion and empathy require listening and generosity of time.

Time is a finite commodity we cherish and protect. Many of us would rather donate money as an act of kindness instead of giving our time. Giving of time seems to be one of the most generous acts of kindness, as we unselfishly take our attention away from other priorities. We can share our time to listen, assist, educate, inspire, and encourage others to become better and reach higher.

Generosity nourishes our values, heart, and soul to see others on an even plane instead of allowing our ego to see us as looking down. This balance of humility taught by spirituality enlightens us to a greater appreciation of others so that we can generously share acts of kindness for the betterment of all. Be generous with the teachings of spirituality.

Humanity has been and will continue to be best served by the generosity of everyone, including you. Generosity begins when you take the initiative to affirm its positive, powerful impact on us all.

YOUR NOTES

List those things for which you give thanks.

Would you say you have the capacity and the willingness to forgive?

Is there someone you should forgive? If so, why are you waiting?

List your last five acts of kindness.

PART 3

OUR SYMPHONY

We are the conductors of life's symphony. Let us discover the beauty of our instruments to play the music to raise the spirit and taste the beauty of life. This section offers the music to inspire us and to inspire others. Through our music, we can encourage those around us and change lives for the better.

LIFE'S NOTE 17

The Beauty of Children

From pregnancy to birth, a baby is a miracle. For most, this is a time of joy. For others, because of overwhelming situations, birth may be a time of mixed emotions. God be with them and embrace them with the strength to provide love and care for an innocent child who depends on them. God's miracle of birth is a blessing. God blesses us as parents to love, nurture, and support this child until death do us part. This baby is a new son or daughter, brother or sister, niece or nephew, grandson or granddaughter. Think of the beauty, love, and joy this baby brings to the world.

> **Inspiration**
>
> The birth of a child is a miracle. Love and cherish each new miracle.

This bundle of joy may be the one who inspires others to follow a life of goodness with meaning and purpose, the one who accomplishes great things, the next great peacemaker, the scientist who discovers benefits for all of humanity, the one who teaches us to dream and imagine. A baby is a gift for the family as well as a gift for the community and humanity. Treasure this miracle of birth and bundle of joy, as there is no copy. Who knows, this may be your only or last child. Give thanks each and every day for God's blessing.

Last night, our second grandson was born. The anticipation and the first sight of him inspired us to once again appreciate and give thanks for the miracle of birth. He touched and inspired me to think more deeply and further cherish this baby's gift and share my thoughts with this note. Moments after birth, a child inspires, reminding and teaching us to be kinder, appreciative, compassionate, and loving. What a beautiful gift!

Our first grandchild, this baby's big brother, has been teaching us and filling us with loving moments for almost four years. His baby brother is fortunate to have such a loving and caring brother. Of course, there will be the typical sibling tussles with "It wasn't me; I didn't do it." However, with their parents' proven approach of loving, caring, and patience, the brothers should have the everlasting closeness of brotherly love. This sibling bond is yet another gift from God.

For those who adopt a child, this too is a gift of rebirth for both the child and the parents. The joy is no less. The miracle of family and love is no less. Adoption illuminates our unselfish capacity for heart expansion and love. The child is the miracle. Adoption is God's blessing. My respect and love for all who have adopted a child. God bless all.

Thanks to my wife for being a wonderful mother and grandma. Our three children, two grandsons, and daughter-in-law have blessed us with a cornucopia of goodness to last a lifetime. Lucky for us, they will continually add to this horn of plenty. Our future is exciting, with new golden moments to be shared, more reasons to give thanks, additional reminders for compassion and goodness, and endless opportunities to share love. We are blessed and give thanks to God.

LIFE'S NOTE 18

Inspire Others to Inspire Self

We all have the opportunity and the ability to offer inspiration for creative thought and action. Many of us are hesitant to inspire others, as we find it either overwhelming or problematic. Common thought is that inspiration must originate from extraordinary stories of conquering difficult challenges. In fact, inspiration is simple encouragement to stimulate motivation for creative perspectives on overcoming life's obstacles and achieving higher levels of accomplishment.

> **Tip**
>
> Initiating support and encouragement is the foundation of inspiration.

Follow the inspirational concept of encouragement to kindly offer words and examples to motivate others to greater heights. Thinking back on who encouraged you to do better can help you appreciate the impact of inspiration. Also, recall when and how that encouragement was expressed. Use these examples to get started encouraging others, giving them a fresh perspective to achieve greater satisfaction and goodness. If for some reason you have yet to be the beneficiary of inspiration, you have before you the opportunity to inspire yourself by inspiring others. Try on inspiration. One size fits all.

Offering inspiration goes beyond any sense of obligation. Encouraging others is, simply put, the right thing to do. Life's goodness is incomplete if we continue to stay on the sidelines as spectators, watching our peers do the work of inspiration. Give inspiration a shot to feel the medicinal benefits of inspiring others and ourselves. Be aware that there are side effects of optimism and positivity leading to satisfaction and joy.

Inspiration is easier than it sounds. Keep it simple, using courtesy and gentle actions to motivate others. Inspiration need not be extraordinary. Stick to the concept of simple encouragement. The act of inspiration is a gift to be shared. Inspiration is lighting someone's candle.

Be Someone's Sunshine

Imagine what we could achieve, both individually and collectively, if we embraced the concept that we can be the sunshine to brighten others' days, even if for only a moment. Share your gifts and share your warmth. Take the initiative to feel the transformative power of goodness and spread it to those around you. Share your sunshine.

> **Tip**
>
> Today comes only once; reach out to brighten someone's day.

How do you brighten someone's day? Initiate engagement with an enthusiastic smile coupled with a warm, friendly greeting to acknowledge another's presence. Consider rekindling the art of kindness with words and actions. The important step is to be the spark, the energy, to light up that person's day. Once you've done so, wait for a reaction. If you continue to talk about yourself, you may appear to be self-centered instead of genuine. Engagement involves complimenting, asking questions, and listening with honest appreciation. After someone has shared a story with you, ask him or her to call you later to tell you more about it. Or better yet, ask if you can call later to hear more. You are probably thinking nobody does this, as we are all too busy. It only takes a moment to reach out. This small act expresses genuine interest and caring. It's not necessary to be a close friend to do this—although it is a great way to make a new friend. Do you have too many friends?

Usually we wait for others to ask for assistance by saying, for example, "Can you help me move this?" or "Can you babysit for me?" or "Do you know someone who can fix this?" or "Can you be a volunteer?" Instead of waiting, anticipate the question and offer to help with the move, babysit, make a repair, or volunteer. The gift of offering your time and effort is powerful and sure to be remembered. When we're asked to help, we're usually conditioned to say no before we even consider the opportunity before us to do good. This doesn't mean to say you should feel obligated to offer every time. Just offer more often.

Kindness seems to have faded some in our daily lives. Make a conscious effort to do small things like noticing something about other people with a positive comment, giving them a small gift to say thank you, and telling them how much you appreciate them. Use your imagination.

Recently while at the checkout at a Walgreens, I was taking more than my share of time. There was only one person behind me in line, a woman who was so patient that upon receiving my change, I gave her a dollar and said, "Thank you for being so kind." She reacted like she had just won the lottery. She was in disbelief and unsure of what to say. After gathering herself, she said, "No one has ever done anything so nice like that for me, thank you so much." I am not sure who brightened whose day more.

Use your imagination to think of your own unique ways to shine your light to brighten and warm the days of others. Consider these ways to be someone's sunshine:

- Greet others with an enthusiastic, warm smile.
- Listen intently to others' thoughts and feelings.
- Initiate conversation with genuine interest.
- Invite someone to join you for a meal or coffee.
- Include others from outside your usual circle in your day.
- Visit those who are sick or shut-in.
- Tell others how much you appreciate them.
- Compliment others with thoughts from your heart.
- Ask to help others with a task.
- Randomly offer to buy someone a drink at a convenience store.
- Enthusiastically share your positive spirit to pick others up.

LIFE'S NOTE 20

Golden Moments

Given the topic, you might expect this note to address the golden years or aging. The focus instead narrows in on creating opportunities for gatherings, celebrations, or simpler get-togethers to be so positive and engraved so deeply in the heart as to be golden moments remembered forever.

Creating golden moments is entirely up to us. We needn't wait for others to initiate. A golden moment is created when we present or organize an event with an impact that is unexpected or reaches beyond normal expectations. Being out of the ordinary, it sparks attention and endearment from the recipients of this moment of kindness.

> **Advice**
>
> A touching moment sparkles brighter than a milestone and endures.

Usually a golden moment involves imagination, creativity, or a pinch of craziness. You will need to think beyond the ordinary for an idea to astound others and knock their socks off. Playing it safe or being afraid of embarrassment limits us and could prevent us from experiencing and sharing a golden moment. At least take a chance to learn by trial and error. We will immediately know when something is a golden moment, as the reaction of the recipient is so intense, with magnified happiness or awe beyond the accustomed response.

Taking our folks to a fancy, exquisite restaurant to celebrate their thirty-fifth wedding anniversary was such a moment. We arranged to have their names on a reserved table with an anniversary celebration card and wine at the table. Seven courses, a musical serenade, and three hours of memories and laughter made this a golden moment to be remembered. My folks fondly talked about this evening for years. Special occasions of celebration are opportunities to engrave a memory of gold.

Our parents' fiftieth, or golden, wedding anniversary was yet another celebration deserving special attention. This included renting a limousine complete with wine, cheese, crackers, and grapes, followed by an elegant meal and a small briefcase containing five hundred-one dollar bills. The moments remembered most were the bananas Foster for dessert and ordering drinks at a fast-food restaurant from a limousine.

Approximately thirty years ago, my sister was the recipient of a soaring golden moment. Our Christmas gift to her was a gift certificate in a colorful envelope. She never expected or would have guessed what was inside. Her reaction upon removing the certificate was immediate panic; she had difficulty breathing and nearly fainted. I think seeing the words "hot-air balloon ride" may have initiated her response. It would have been helpful if I had previously heard her say, "I'm afraid of heights." The balloon guy was kind enough to refund the money. In place of a balloon ride, she bought a dresser. My sister still gets nervous when she receives a gift from us in an envelope.

Yet another golden moment happened while we were traveling with our three young children to my wife's parents' house. We arrived after midnight, the morning of my wife's birthday. To be the first to celebrate her birthday, the kids and I had baked and decorated a cake and hid it under the backseat in the van, to be revealed at the stroke of midnight. At midnight, we sang "Happy Birthday", which she didn't expect, and when she turned to see the children singing she saw her cake with one unlit candle. (The use of a lighted candle in a motor vehicle is not recommended.) She was so happy and touched that she cried with joy. She continues to recall this kindness with a big smile and watery eyes.

Valentine's Day 2013 was a gold-medal golden moment. I had done flowers, candy, jewelry, and lingerie before. My mind was a blank, with no idea of what to do this year. I wanted to do something that would express my love and wow my wife. Weeks before, she mentioned how much she enjoyed the group the Piano Guys on YouTube. Two guys make up the group: a piano guy and a cello guy. She was so mesmerized with the sound resonating from the cello. She said, "Someday, I would like to learn to play the cello." I remembered her words and immediately thought, *This is it. This is an opportunity to make a dream come true.* My wife had also commented that we should celebrate Valentine's Day on multiple days rather than only one day.

Nine days before Valentine's Day, I rented a new cello from the Band Store, complete with case, bow, and rosin. The anticipation and excitement was too much, so I gave it to her on February 5. I hugged her and said, "Valentine's Day starts today and last for two weeks." I asked her to sit down and close her eyes. With the cello before her, I asked her to open her eyes. She was speechless and looked as if she would faint. After composing herself, she mumbled, "I can't do this. How much did it cost? I don't know how to play." I reminded her of her affection for the Piano Guys and what she had said about someday playing the cello. I said, "Your someday is today. Have fun with it." She had her first lesson on February 23 and continues with lessons. She is excited and is giving it a hearty go. The family anxiously awaits her home recital.

The most recent golden moment was a day after the birth of our second grandson. His older brother for months leading up to the birth had referred to his soon-to-be brother with fond loving names: "Pancake," "Appletree," "Hamburger," and "Pasta." We all loved these names throughout his mom's pregnancy. To capture this history I did four drawings on a white poster board, capturing each of the beloved names of endearment. Moments after birth, the parents introduced to us our second grandson. His name, birthdate, weight, and length were then added to the poster with some drawings from his older brother. Our son told us this was the most cherished gift, and it will be framed to record history.

Ideas to Inspire Golden Moments

- Fix a home dinner with candles, wine, and flowers for no expected reason.
- Prepare a schedule of surprise events for a full day from morning to night when the two of you do things the other enjoys.
- Write a poem.
- Paint a picture, make a piece of pottery, do a carving, or sing a song.
- Plan a surprise gathering of friends.
- Surprise someone with tickets to an event.
- Schedule a day at the spa for the two of you, a hot-air balloon ride, skydiving, or a surprise flight for a short getaway.
- Take a limousine ride, plan a surprise family gathering, bake a two-foot-tall celebration cake, take a hike in the woods, or surprise someone at work with a catered lunch for two.

The ideas for golden moments are limited only by our imagination. Have fun, enjoy, and remember them forever. Be thankful you took the initiative to surprise and touch someone so deeply. That person will be forever grateful for the moment of gold.

LIFE'S NOTE 21

Dream Bigger to Reach Higher

Dream often and dream big. Because research shows that when waking up we usually cannot remember our sleeping dreams, the focus of this note will be on dreaming of hopes and aspirations while awake. With the many distractions of daily life, learn to record your dreams in writing for future reference and inspiration.

> **Tip**
>
> Dream beyond the clouds, for the impossible to be possible.

Often we see hanging from the rearview mirror of an automobile an ornate circular design with beads, feathers, and wrapping called a *dream catcher*. Its significance is not about the quantity of dreams caught, but what we do to make the dreams we catch come true. What is important with a dream catcher is the way it reminds us to dream often and dream big.

Dreaming invigorates excitement and energy to formulate a plan of action. Anticipation of the possibilities of achieving a dream fills us with enthusiasm and lifts our spirit. Hope cultivates the seeds of dreams to be watered and nurtured. With effort, they will take root, grow, and blossom.

Dreams are necessary to create a constant stream of inspiration ending in action. Without dreams, all this is lost. Contentment begins to settle in, imagination diminishes, and motivation lessens. We become lackadaisical, losing interest and allowing a dull boring spirit to lead us to days of inactivity. Dreaming energizes our mind and heart to look beyond our potential and grasp more than we would have thought possible.

It is not a stretch to conclude that those who don't dream miss their potential in life, while dreamers reach and grasp the fruit of their dreams with gusto, achieving their potential and beyond. Dreams contribute to enthusiasm, positive personality, and attitude, with others wanting to associate with us and be around us. Imagine life without dreams. How dull and lonely it would be! Dream to be enthusiastic and energetic, and you will not be lonely.

Share your dreams with others. Some may laugh or think you're a little crazy. If so, they have confirmed that you are dreaming big and reaching for the stars. Who knows, they may have a similar dream or share a dream that triggers an idea to follow and achieve your own dream. If you find another with the same dream, consider teaming up to experience it together.

Dreams come in all shapes and sizes. Once you have a dream, write it down to acknowledge that this dream is important to you. Periodically review your list of dreams to spike your imagination and energy and fully enjoy your experience of catching and living your dream.

LIFE'S NOTE 22

Kaleidoscope of Imagination

Imagine our world without imagination. There would be no books, music, theater, movies, paintings, sculptures, artwork, architecture, inventions, exploration, or discovery—and no Disney. Our lives would be influenced by limitations and a repetitive structure void of exciting and inspiring ideas and experiences of newness.

Imagination shapes our freedom to think beyond conventional and conceived limitations. To imagine is to dream the

> **Vision**
>
> Imagination is kaleidoscope thinking beyond the possible to limitless possibilities.

impossible. Think how the course of history would have been altered if Thomas Edison or Benjamin Franklin had given in to perceived limitations and not imagined beyond. Countless sticks of chalk have been used by physicists, astronomers, and mathematicians to calculate and imagine what is beyond. Even the laws of physics are challenged, with possibly the discovery of new laws or the altering of existing ones. There will be new thinkers to continue the works of Newton, Einstein, and Hawking. Limiting imagination only limits further discovery.

Imagination is the engine that expands the mind to wonder

1. What if . . . ?
2. How can . . . ?
3. Why not . . . ?
4. Who will . . . ?
5. Where will . . . ?
6. Will it . . . ?

These six simple questions form the dreamy kaleidoscope of imagination. For example, how can we cut grass better and in less time? Why not have self-cleaning dishes or a house with movable interior walls? With imagination, we realize no matter what it is, it can always be improved. Imagination feeds our wonderment and determination to never give up. Who determines the limits of possibility? We could be the ones who make it possible. Imagine those who have heard, "You will never walk again," and then imagine that someday they will—and they do. Imagination drives motivation, determination, and the will to never give up to achieve your goals.

The power of imagination is the ability to visualize images in high definition and replay for expansion and refinement. Record your ideas on paper, including the basic principle to recall for future reference and enhanced imagination. We all have the capacity to imagine, no matter how simple or how crazy our ideas may be. Do not discount the possibility of an idea or thought. Over time, it might all make sense and be realized.

Daily imagination exercises the mind to think beyond, to be creative and dream. Combine imagination, creativity, and dreaming to expand your scope and begin to comprehend and understand that what was once unobtainable or unreachable is now possible. You'll feel better with expanded energy and enthusiasm that you can achieve and experience what you thought was merely a hope. Incorporating imagination into your life directs your focus away from an attitude of *that would never happen* to optimism that it is possible. Replacing doubtful, even negative, thought is possible when you use your imagination to redirect to positivity and belief.

Ideas to Spark Imagination

- Think of a new game.
- Make a super-comfortable recliner double as a bed.
- Try a new food recipe.
- Ask *What if? Why not?* and *How can I improve?*
- Plan new activities to draw the family together.
- Strategize a way to recover from a tough life challenge.
- Bring relief to those in pain and suffering.
- Think of better ways to help caregivers.
- Develop more efficient teaching methods.
- Improve study methods.

LIFE'S NOTE 23

Mother Nature's Canvas and Playground

The gift of nature is a canvas unlike any other, to be appreciated and treasured. Nature is also the biggest and grandest playground. Discover and explore its majestic beauty and inspiration. The doors to nature's theme parks are always open. There is no minimum height requirement or fee for this lifelong ride.

Nature's playground offers adventures in hiking, swimming, bicycling, walking along paths, or blazing your own trail to enjoy nature's stunning beauty and tranquility. Pause to enjoy the seasonal transformation painting a new canvas of your favorite paths and settings. Appreciate nature's grand scale as well as the balance of the ecosystem contributing to your health. When moms speak, people listen. Listen to Mother Nature to protect and preserve its beauty for generations.

All of our senses will be invigorated from a day outside among the sights, smells, sounds, textures, and tastes of nature. The color palette, brushstrokes, sculptures, flow, and contrasts all combine for high-definition pictures of magnificence and imagination found only in nature. Wildflowers, trees, grasses, soil, and water all blend together for the fragrance only nature offers. Trees are the woodwind section of nature's symphony. Breezes and wind are the string section. Birds and animals are the horn and percussion sections. Enjoy the melody of their music. Nature has a bounty of textures, from the sandpaper roughness of a pinecone to the softness of a spring leaf, from the contoured peaks and valleys of a tree's bark to the the smoothness of a flower's petals. Nature's cafe has desserts of wild blueberries, strawberries, and blackberries, and snacks of dandelion root, some mushrooms, and nuts. No napkin, manners, or etiquette are necessary. We are free to chew with our mouth open as we relish the tastes and aromas of nature's sensory blend.

> *Inspiration*
>
> *Mother Nature paints and composes the world's largest art show. Enjoy and appreciate its beauty.*

Relax and be still to quietly scan the flowing landscape and appreciate its complexity and simplicity. Lie on your back in an opening to look upward at the trees and sky. Feel the texture of the ground, the grass, and the leaves. Be aware of a breeze softly touching your face. Watch the graceful swaying of tree branches. Listen to the gentle rustling of leaves. See the squirrels scurrying from branch to branch. Be amazed how birds avoid twigs and leaves to effortlessly perch on a branch. Look beyond the trees skyward to appreciate the puffy, floating white clouds, the color of the sky, and the birds soaring to heights only we can imagine. Wonder how all this awe-inspiring synchronization of nature came to be.

We must get back to spending more time outside and less on computers, video games, TV, tweeting, or texting. Nature is a live video game in 3D and HD, inspiring expressions of appreciation and gratitude for the privilege of being a part of its grandeur. A day outdoors, full of fresh air and activity, is nature's natural sedative for a good night's sleep.

Appreciation

Trees are the woodwind section of nature's symphony; appreciate their music.

LIFE'S NOTE 24

Taste the Adrenaline of Adventure

Life without adventure is mundane and boring. Reach inside to awaken your sense of adventure. We all have in our genes the desire to seek and explore adventure. Weigh the level of risk to fit your personality and comfort zone. High risk for one may be nothing for another. Adventure is your journey to experience and growth.

> **Quote**
>
> *Adventure is to taste the sizzle of life's gourmet cuisine.*

Dare to push the envelope slightly beyond where you have never gone. Taste the adrenaline rush and invigorating excitement of living your dreams, hopes, and far-flung risky desires. Before pursuing an adventure, research, prepare, and train if necessary to minimize risk and maximize safety. Adventures should be fun, not terrorizing and debilitating. Memories of adventures should be fond and a little crazy.

We all have to define for ourselves what constitutes an adventure. Avoid the mistake of letting others influence your definition. Stay true to yourself to enjoy and magnify the experience. Adventures run the gamut from skydiving to taking a painting class, from scuba diving to hiking up a hill. The purpose of adventure is to try to experience new things to expand your horizons, meet new people along the way, and possibly make new friends.

Adventure can be spontaneous if the risk is minimal and the fun level is high. For example, if you're a fair-weather person, you may decide to take a walk during heavy snowfall and chilling cold. Big snowflakes alight on your nose and cheeks. Your glasses fog up. You wipe them to see the beauty of the moment, and enjoy the reward of a cup of hot chocolate and marshmallows waiting at home. Or maybe getting dirty and muddy is not in your vocabulary, but you decide on a hot summer day to walk with a friend in a shallow stream, discovering the beauty of nature from a fresh perspective. Excitement and the feeling of accomplishment and satisfaction are the results of measured exploration to discover and awaken untapped energy within.

Risk-takers have a thirst to dare more, reach further, and challenge themselves for greater rush and reward. They must calculate risk after extensive preparation and training instead of acting with spontaneity. Scuba diving, skydiving, and rock climbing are examples of hazardous endeavors. Placing lives at risk requires cautious preparation and extensive training to measure the difficulty of targeted risky events and adventures.

To inspire and encourage adventure, refer to the list of examples below. Next to the ones that appeal to you, write your ideas for pursuing this adventure. Energize your spirit to explore and discover.

Ideas for Adventure

- Order something other than the usual at a restaurant.
- Try a new restaurant.
- Go snow skiing or waterskiing.
- Enroll in a night class for writing, pottery, painting, or whatever appeals to you.
- Take swim or scuba lessons at the YMCA.
- Go bungee jumping.
- Plant a garden.
- Try skydiving.
- Take a cooking class.
- Run a 10K or marathon.
- Do sprint triathlons.
- Learn woodworking.
- Do some public speaking.
- Become a life coach or personal trainer.
- Volunteer.
- Step outside your daily routine.
- Try fishing.
- Go camping.
- Ride a bicycle.
- Surprise someone with a party or event.
- Share your goals and dreams.

- Learn to play a musical instrument.
- Paddle a kayak or canoe.

Let adventure ignite your spirit to go beyond your self-proclaimed limits.

LIFE'S NOTE 25

Enthusiasms Come from Within

Enthusiasms are multiple activities, situations, and things about which we are enthusiastic. An enthusiasm goes beyond an interest. Examples of enthusiasms include family, hobbies, sports, music, movies, theater, the outdoors, spirituality, volunteering, and career. These are things that go beyond creating normal energy, excitement, enjoyment, and passion, or are near and dear to your heart. Enthusiasms are things that energize your spirit to eagerly share with others.

> **Tip**
>
> *Enthusiasms are the sprinkles and sparkles that energize life.*

It is in our human nature to be energetic and enthusiastic. We strive to overcome any obstacles that keep us from fanning the flames of enthusiasm and sharing our enthusiasms. We all benefit from listening to others' stories told in the contagious, intoxicating excitement of inspiring enthusiasm. The best vaccination for negativity is having enthusiasms to initiate and feed positivity and enthusiastic living.

We are the only one limiting our enthusiasms. When we do that, we also limit our growth and potential. Without limits, imagine how enthusiastic we could be and how we could enhance the energy and enjoyment we feel in our lives. Living unenthusiastic, dull, boring days means we're missing opportunities for happiness and a fulfilling, energetic life. Do your best not to be the person who merely exists. Start now and discover your enthusiasms. Enjoy your newfound enthusiasms and the rewards of energy and happiness they bring.

Enthusiasms are an ever-evolving carousel to explore, discover, and initiate new enthusiasms for freshness in life. Light from new enthusiasms illuminates new pathways to follow for new scenery and personal discovery. Situations arise from life's detours and intersections, changing the course of life as existing enthusiasms flare and fade away. Be keenly aware of the possibilities as you recognize and visualize potential new enthusiasms and continually add enthusiasms for a fun, happy, and positive life. Begin today to explore the potential benefits of enthusiasms for your own happiness as well as that of your family and friends. Enthusiasm is infectious and contagious. This is a good thing.

LIFE'S NOTE 26

The Art of Sport

Arts and sports share some common characteristics, and each has its place. They share a need for a high degree of interest and hours of practice. Participation in both should build confidence and self-esteem as well as coordination. Both teach us to push ourselves to achieve more in life.

> **Tip**
>
> Appreciate the beauty and teachings of art and sport.

Colleges have a comparable number of students participating in the arts as in athletics. Sports, especially football, will always claim their significance to a school by generating the revenue to subsidize all other student activities. Unique to the arts are students learning to dream, imagine, and be creative, as well as gaining the sense of order, structure, and discipline shared by sports. Other benefits of the arts include broader awareness, appreciation, and profound thought about all within and surrounding us.

As youngsters, we gravitate more toward sports than the arts, either on our own accord or at the prodding of our parents. Some parents encourage their children to participate in sports because they want to live vicariously through their children. Many parents believe their child is the next great athlete, destined for athletic scholarships. It's wise to temper those expectations and be more realistic, as a majority of children for various reasons or physical limitations do not reach a high enough level of athleticism to advance. Congratulations to those who do achieve success or are genetically gifted.

For the safety of your children, consider that athletes are major contributors to the success of orthopedic clinics. Some athletes, specifically of contact sports, later in life pay the price of constant pain or impaired mobility. This is not to say that sports are bad. Just be aware of the greater risks associated with some sports. Are the risks worth the rewards?

Fear of failure is a common thread for both the arts and sports. Usually, with sports, the fear of failure identifies itself earlier on than in the arts. Coaches of youth sports teach the fundamentals. However, most also teach the importance of winning. As children get older, winning becomes the only thing that matters, skewing their perspective of the building blocks for well-being. Players become labeled by level of achievement and athleticism. Some have now made a select team. Belief in self is built up for some but eroded for others.

The arts are more supportive, patient, and forgiving. Whereas there is a designated period of time in life to excel at sports followed by a noticeable decline in skills, the arts offer longevity as well as a lifelong hobby. Few sports—golf, tennis, running, walking, swimming—offer the same sort of longevity. Some may argue that physically working out qualifies as a sport. It does offer some longevity, but it is not a sport. However, continued physical activity has shown to contribute to overall health.

Parents who share their interest in the arts and expose their children to the arts early in life take advantage of an opportunity to generate a child's interest. To encourage athletic interest, we play sports with our children in the backyard or on a court or field. Balance this exposure for equal time with the arts. Children react positively to music, film, dance, and other artistic pursuits. Do what you can to increase that interest and make it an enduring one. Play music around the house, dance with your children, make videos of their plays and shows, and take them to musical and theatrical events.

The arts—including painting, singing, pottery, sculpting, writing, poetry, and music—are all subjective, with beauty being in the eye of the artist and the beholder. You might not see or appreciate the beauty in a particular work of art, while another might appreciate its symbolism and story. Most arts develop a blend of auditory, visual, and hand-eye coordination. If you doubt this, try playing a musical instrument. You will quickly see that learning any of the arts can be a difficult endeavor. Being patient, persistent, and persevering not only improves your artistic skills but teaches you these same lessons to cope with life's situations and challenges. Encourage interest in the arts for lifelong lessons and a lifelong hobby.

With the arts, it is never too late to start. Discover the compatibility of the arts and sports to invigorate your life and sustain your well-being. Your mind, spirit, and physicality are all influenced and motivated by the arts and sports. Appreciate the beauty of both.

LIFE'S NOTE 27

A Bigger Bucket List

E nergize yourself by creating a bucket list filled with hopes and dreams. Items on your list can be a combination of realistic obtainable activities and challenging or far-reaching things to do. Variety in the items on your list encourages you to experience those activities and place check marks of accomplishment and satisfaction next to each item. Continue to add new and fresh things to your list. Reach for and experience your hopes and dreams.

Bucket lists feed our imagination and wonderment, encouraging us to dream bigger and achieve great things. Anticipation of events and activities injects enthusiasm and excitement along with planning for the experience and completion of a dream on your bucket list. The weeks of research, preparation, and planning to fulfill a dream can be as exhilarating as living the dream itself.

Buy a metal bucket or pail and decorate it to suit your personality. Fill it with pictures, notes, and stuff to create your list. Put the bucket in a place of prominence as a daily reminder to encourage an enthusiastic journey to experience your dreams.

Fill your bucket to lift your spirit and feed your passion to discover realms that exceed your current boundaries, reaching above and beyond what you thought possible. Your bucket is the fuel to awaken your adventurous spirit to relish unique experiences. The ultimate reward is in taking the risk of becoming so involved in your dreams and taking action to live them out. Once you've checked off an item, buy and design a "Completed" bucket for notes, pictures, and stuff relating to that dream to look back on for satisfaction and inspiration. Enthusiastically mark this day of transformation with jubilant ceremony for having been a spectator and living the dream.

Possible Bucket-List Hopes and Dreams

- skydiving
- bungee jumping
- scuba diving
- running a marathon
- participating in a triathlon
- learning to play a musical instrument
- taking voice lessons
- taking dance lessons
- public speaking
- establishing a nonprofit or support group
- taking cooking lessons
- writing a book
- traveling to places that were only dreams
- changing careers
- writing a book

LIFE'S NOTE 28

Laughter Is Contagious

L aughter is the universal language, easily recognizable around the world. Words often trace their origin and roots to the Greeks, and so it is with the study of laughter, *gelotology*. The origin is the Greek word *gelos*. *Gelos* looks so similar to *gelatin*, *Jell-O*, and *jelly*. all with a jiggly wiggly connotation. I like to imagine a scholarly group of Greeks sipping tankards of ale around a fire pit telling stories. Suddenly, bellies began to jiggle and mouths gape open uttering *hee hees*, *hah hahs*, and *ho hos*. A wise person says, "We need to study this behavior, and it needs a name." The word receiving the most votes? *Gelotology*.

> **Tip**
>
> Laughter is daily doses of happy. Laugh loud and often.

Studies repeatedly reveal that laughter is good medicine. Laughter's physiological benefits include relief of pain and less stress, all contributing to a warmer heart and a healthier you.

We break out in laughter as a response to various stimuli, such as stories, thoughts, humor, tickling, and embarrassment. Being the victim of a prank is an example of an embarrassing situation that spurs selfish laughter from the instigators. Pranking, though admittedly funny, must be measured with consideration for the safety of and the emotional impact on the one being pranked. Going too far is certainly not worth a moment of laughter at the detriment of someone else. Most of us enjoy hiding to suddenly startle someone. However, using flour, syrup, or a surprise punch is going too far. In addition, any attempt to create laughter at others' expense by embarrassing or insulting them is poor judgment and disrespectful.

We also experience situations of chance causing embarrassment. Ripped pants or food on our face are two trivial examples. At one time or another, we all have goofy things happen to us. Instead of being uptight and so prim and proper, the best solution is to learn to laugh at yourself to defuse a potentially embarrassing situation. Healthier opportunities for laughter come from gathering around to play games, tell stories, and reminisce. Silliness has a way of initiating crazy laughter. Have a theme party, play silly word games, or do crazy made-up stuff. Laugh-a-thons are contagious, creating ideas for future laugh-a-thon opportunities. Don't be afraid to get goofy.

As we age, the need for laughter becomes more apparent, as the stress of facing life's challenges drags us down. Adults have more stories and experiences than children to initiate laughter, yet we laugh far less than children. Many would probably agree that we need more laughter as we age and become cynical.

How we laugh is funny in and of itself. The giggler laughs with high-pitched quick sounds in a silly or nervous way. Chucklers express a soft low-toned laugh. Chortlers utter a gleeful chuckling or snorting sound. Most unique is the cackler, who makes shrill broken sounds like a hen. Belly laughers bring the gusto of a hearty laugh, infecting others to laugh. Tearful laughers are moved so deeply that their eyes water and their body physically hurts from intense prolonged laughter. Place all these types of laughers together for a symphonic medley of joy. Listening to our silly sounds helps to understand the contagious effects of laughter, promoting more laughter and a healthier us. Share the laughter.

YOUR NOTES

Describe the last time you inspired or encouraged someone.

Describe how someone inspired you.

What do you see and how do you feel when you lie in the grass on your back looking skyward?

PART 4

The moment we're born, we're a member of the family. The hope is that each of us had and continues to have a strong family relationship. As we all know, family relationships can be affected and stressed by numerous challenges. Societal changes and family dynamics are addressed in this section to help us better appreciate our parents and siblings as well as our extended family of relatives. Ideas are offered for expressing gratitude and grasping the magnificence of family. Time is of the essence, and these notes illustrate how we can better use our time together.

LIFE'S NOTE 29

Family Endurance: It's a Marathon

Millions have marveled at the majestic carvings of the Grand Canyon, the mystery and music of Niagara Falls, the vastness and spectacular sights of Yellowstone National Park, the reliability of Old Faithful, the power and meandering beauty of the Mississippi River, and the sturdiness and longevity of the towering trees in Sequoia National Park. Families embody the same awe-inspiring attributes as nature's wonders, along with love, resiliency, and a tight bond felt only within a family. Friends may come and go, but family should always be there.

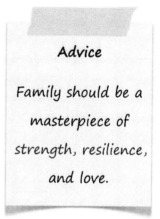

Advice

Family should be a masterpiece of strength, resilience, and love.

Families persevere through times of struggle, upheaval, loss, devastation, and sorrow to remain intact with love, support, compassion, and forgiveness. The family is much like nature, always adapting to unfavorable conditions to persist and survive, becoming stronger with deeper connections. Families do not give in and do not give up. The bond of the family relationship is unlike any other with its ability to bend and not break.

Family trees go back centuries without being uprooted. They may have swayed from stress in the past, causing a minor crack. However, they self-healed and continued to grow to welcome new members into the family. The birth of a baby brings awe and inspiration to light the fire of love and passion to care for, protect, and teach a fresh new face.

The strength of a family grows from years of close connection, solidified by the familiarity of day-to-day routine. Order provides stability and comfort for harmony and balance. This cultivates dependability—no matter how much the tree is shaken, the family flourishes. Resiliency of family to recover from challenges ties the family together with the belief that this intimate bond will be there to support and love us forever. As time and life's experiences pass by, a unity of oneness develops, with each family member having a true feeling of belonging. Family is our place of comfort to thrive and grow.

Unfortunately, there are families that do not have the strength or have lost the strength to nurture and endure as a result of tumultuous forces eroding the family order to the point of disruption and negativity. Forces dividing or breaking families apart, sad to say, are many, including divorce, addiction, trauma, disease, finances, job loss, loss of status, sense of failure, and verbal, physical, sexual, or emotional abuse. If this describes your family, do not give in to despair and hopelessness. You may feel lonely and confused, with little if any hope to once again have happiness and connection. Family boundaries must be redefined.

Acceptance and taking ownership of your challenges with family are the initial steps to reestablishing a feeling of belonging. This may mean restoring and preserving the family as before or different, with an effort to cultivate relationships within the family. We may need to rely on friends, and the friends we make can be our new family. The size of family is far less important than the relationship between family members. Your new family might be you and one other person. If so, celebrate and nurture this relationship to deepen the bond until it approaches that of family. Your situation might be different from the past but better than the disruptive atmosphere of before.

If you have been freed from an abusive family situation, give thanks and take the initiative, as difficult as it may be, to pick yourself up to move forward. Begin by taking baby steps that lead to significant progress toward your goal of reconnecting to restore order and comfort. Restoring love might take more time than expected before you once again feel accepted and appreciated just as you are. You are at one of life's detours, so choose your path wisely. You can choose a path of despair and anger, guilt and pity, depression, or living in the past and allowing it to control your future. Or you can choose a path of a fresh beginning with positive situations and goals to inspire the will and strengthen self-esteem to better your life. Or you can choose to do nothing, give up, and succumb to the grasp of your constricting situation. The choice is yours. The road will be difficult, with pitfalls along the way. Do not give up. Be patient and persevere, as who knows which corner you might turn to bring back smiles, laughter, and purpose to restore happiness, love, and meaning.

Harmony among everyone in any family can be trying at times. We argue, fight, verbally attack, embarrass, and shame each other. This close, confined connection of day to day intimacy threatens harmony and, if allowed, contributes to inexcusable negative behavior. Why do we say and do things to brothers and sisters or parents that we would not consider appropriate for friends and acquaintances? If left unchecked, closeness and intimacy begin to feel suffocating, and we challenge family members while we grow to be our own person. Trust that with time, patience, understanding, and forgiveness, harmony and balance will once again be the norm.

Communication is paramount for a harmonious and loving family. Sound communication is a two-way street. The core of caring communication is an attitude of *we* and *us* rather than *I* and *me*. The habit of selfishly thinking about *I* and *me* shuts down other family members to a position of no longer listening and caring. Communication is hindered as we think we are the only one in the car. We talk as loud as we like. Others might hear us, but no one is listening. In essence, we are riding alone.

There is a major difference between hearing and listening. *Hearing* is attention to sound with no true interest. *Listening* is the interpretation of sound with caring thought, emotion, and genuine interest in the other person. Anybody can talk, but listening is an art. Learn and practice the art of listening for solid two-way communication. Be respectful, caring, and interested in others' lives. Families who communicate kindly are honest and respectful with each other, establishing trust and happiness.

Happy, satisfying, respectful, and harmonious families don't just happen. To achieve and maintain this level of comfort requires daily work to hone your skills of tolerance, patience, compassion, perseverance, forgiveness, support, and love. You will be tested, so continually further your craft of family skills to nurture the family to endure forever and be there for one another.

LIFE'S NOTE 30

The Apple Doesn't Fall Far from the Tree

A few months ago, I had a conversation with a female relative whose daughter commented that she would parent differently. This bothered the mom for quite a while to think how she might have failed and what she could have done differently. She had me now evaluating my own parenting skills with raising our three grown children. Upon the birth of our first grandchild, our oldest son said he would parent differently than his mom and I did. Continuing our conversation, my relative shared that she had recently concluded that she had been and continues to be a good and successful parent. Her conclusion came from realizing that her four grown children are all grounded, kind, and loving parents. This is the fruit of her parenting and her reward, of which she is extremely proud. Our children have these same traits of kindness and love. I too am proud and blessed.

> **Advice**
>
> *Children thrive from love and encouragement rather than judgment and criticism.*

A child wanting to parent differently than his or her folks seems natural, as parenting is by no means an easy skill to learn or perfect. Numerous factors and variables impact how we parent, so don't interpret your children wanting to parent differently as a critique or failure. How do we know when we have perfected parenting, and are there any perfect parents? Much has been written about ways to parent. The basics of parenting are tried and true.

However, influences from our ever-changing environment will continue to modify parenting skills. Articles in parenting publications express different views than articles written decades ago, and ones in the future will be different as well. The introduction of social media has certainly changed parenting to a higher level of awareness to protect our children as well as sensitivity for allocation of time.

Technology will continue to challenge moms and dads to adapt their parenting skills.

Parenting is a difficult, challenging responsibility, impacted by numerous outside factors attacking our lessons to our children and putting the outcome of our years of being a responsible loving parent at risk. Unfortunately, these influences can impel a child to rebel and pull away to the point of damaging the parent-child relationship so deeply that it seems to be beyond repair. We question our parenting ability and reflect on what we could have done differently. If you were and are a loving, kind, caring, and responsible parent, and did all that was good, congratulations on a job well done

Parenting with sound best practices does not necessarily result in great kids. However, it dramatically increases the odds of a positive outcome. Similarly, poor parenting does not always mean troubled children, contrary to popular opinion. Some children are more mature than others. They have the internal strength of adaptability and resiliency to survive poor parenting. Do not underestimate the style of parenting, which greatly influences the outcome of good or troubled kids. Sometimes troubled kids do traumatic or horrifying acts. This does not necessarily correlate to their parents being bad parents. There are both overwhelming and overriding outside influences involved, and in some cases luck. Our children may be in the wrong place at the wrong time or in an inspirational setting at just the right time, influencing their life.

Environment contributes greatly to children's upbringing and the lessons learned. Children learn by example, and an environment of negativity, pessimism, substance abuse, constant criticism, judgment, abusive language, and infidelity can lead children to grow hard-hearted and rebellious, or leave them begging for love and compassion. We are no different from animals cuddling and playing with their young ones, teaching them the ways of life. Our young ones require the same cuddling with hugs and kisses, positive support, compassion, and love to become grounded, respectful, responsible, and loving children and adults. The apple does not fall far from the tree.

It may sting when our children strive to parent better than their parents, but it's a desire we do not want to discourage. No matter how excellent or poor our parenting skills, there is always room for improvement. Wanting to improve, and maybe the need to be a better parent, is an admirable and desirable trait to be encouraged. This desire does not necessarily mean we failed as a parent. In fact, it shows that we set an example. Remember, the apple does not fall far from the tree. Nurture and grow a family tree with positive parenting skills.

Positive Parenting Skills

- loving environment
- affection
- saying "I love you"
- appreciation
- encouragement
- acceptance
- caring
- kindness
- including a pet in the family
- responsibility
- commitment to children
- unselfishness with time and involvement
- creating an environment of goodness
- compassion
- forgiveness
- happiness
- positivity
- optimism
- having realistic expectations
- talking with children
- listening to children
- establishing rapport
- leading by example
- teaching the value of volunteering
- teaching right from wrong
- understanding limits and rules
- keeping consequences consistent
- emotional stability in times of stress

> **Tip**
>
> The apple doesn't fall far from the tree, as family grows on the same branch.

- learning to use the positivity of the word *yes* more than the negativity of the word *no*
- trust and respect
- avoiding favoritism and comparisons
- practicing and following all the above for a healthy relationship with your spouse

LIFE'S NOTE 31

Time: Prioritize and Allocate

Careers teach us to schedule time with the use of day planners or electronic scheduling and reminders via computer and smart phone. Continual use of these gadgets for career and social interaction comes at a cost to family, with our obsession to be connected with work in the evening and on weekends. Social media also take away quality time from connecting with family. When using social media at home, we think we are with family. We are with family physically, but absent from shared conversation and connection. Take back ownership of family time for quality relationships, especially for the short eighteen or so years a child lives at home. During this period, subtract from each day hours for sleep, work, and activities away from family to appreciate the precious value of time.

> **Tip**
>
> There is no replacing lost time. Sorry, there are no do-overs.

As youngsters, we are unaware of time, believing we have plenty of it with no sense of urgency or appreciation for its passing. A child graduating from high school, moving away from home, or going to college seems to prompt our initial awareness of the passing of time. The marriage of a son or daughter is another landmark to measure the gravity of time. With the introduction of grandchildren and the continued passing of years, time is finally appreciated as a finite gift to be cherished.

Reflection of life's decades reveals how little time we have available with family and how we actually misallocate our time. We still think there is plenty of time, but we might begin to think we should be obsessed with time passing. The message is to develop an awareness and greater appreciation for time, especially time for family.

There is a difference between time *with* family and time *for* family. Temptations will continue to test our ability to prioritize our time. How simple it is to give in to temptation to be with buddies or attend group activities away from family. We attempt to rationalize our decision by thinking *I will make it up to the family members being impacted.* Yet we do not have the ability to make up or replace lost time. It's true that we all need some solo time to relax and recharge. However, use caution to balance quality of time in favor of family.

When making decisions to choose between family activities, time with buddies, or time alone, get your priorities in order and allocate your time wisely. We prioritize time at work with the assistance of electronic gadgets. Think with life's gadget, your heart, for the needs of your children and spouse. Choose to prioritize and allocate time for both your family and yourself to benefit from loving experiences.

LIFE'S NOTE 32

Social-Media Addiction

Social media, with its unprecedented growth and popularity, has strained the dynamics of family and relationships. During the last ten to twenty years, we have been bombarded with all sorts of electronic gadgets and communication platforms impacting our communication and social skills. Their intoxicating allure—with real-time information, instant gratification, and entertainment—has captured us in an ever-expanding and seductive net.

> **Question**
>
> Do you find the prolific use of social media fostering disconnection rather than connection?

A classic example of the grip social media has on our life is how people react when receiving a text message or a cell-phone call. The common reaction is to, without hesitation, inconsiderately text back or answer the phone. People then think it is acceptable to carry on a conversation while friends or family in attendance wonder and wait. Rudeness like this shows no kindness or consideration for the ones who have chosen to be in our presence. Instead, we accept and in some twisted way believe that allowing a non-present third party to control our time and the time of those in our presence is okay. Our etiquette and priorities have been turned upside down by the phenomenon of social media.

Social media for business has, without question, had a profound impact on increased productivity and efficiency. However, this has come with costs to family and social interaction, weakening relationships. As in business, where we are on our way to becoming robots, family members are following a similar course, with their time now consumed with social media, leaving little for family. Both parents and businesses share the responsibility for these social-media phenomena.

Social media expand the business day outside the brick-and-mortar of the office. The computer and cell phone have permeated family time. Arriving home from a busy work day, we most likely continue to check our messages on our home computer and reply, followed by the same on our cell phone. Our cell phones have taken ownership over us. Take back ownership of your cell phone by setting it on silent mode or, better yet, turning it off when at home. Respond only to emergencies.

Cell phones have evolved into a sixth finger or even a third hand, always in our possession or close by. Think of the feeling of despair and panic we feel when we cannot find our cell phone. Witnessing this reaction firsthand, you would think someone died. Businesses have come to expect and demand that we remain connected 24/7 to be more responsive and productive. No more. Quality time with family comes first. We need to rearrange our priorities for the scale of balance to favor the family.

Parents have set the example of social media busy-ness. Our families are inundated with enough electronic gadgets, controls, and multimedia stuff to open our own store. These all encourage solitary activity, requiring no communication or interaction with the family. On a typical night or weekend at home, sons or daughters are either in their room or curled up in a chair on their cell phone or a computer, and the parents are either doing the same or watching television. There is no communication—or, at best, communication is minimal and shallow. We might hear what is said, but listening is nonexistent.

If you are skeptical, count how many times you hear responses like "huh," "what," "fine," "okay," "sure," or "can you repeat that?" We are more concerned with getting our kids to hang up clothes, put away shoes, clean floors, and keep a neat room than we are with the epidemic use of social media and the costs to the family. Take steps today to prioritize and correct the erosion of quality family time.

The steps for restoring family time are quite simple: Set aside time each week for no use or possession of social media gadgets. Start with a few hours one day a week, or for those with greater vision, a full day on the weekend and one or two nights a week designated for family time. Now there is time to plan and schedule family activities. The types of activities are limited only by your imagination. Ask each family member to volunteer to organize the family activity for the next scheduled family time. This way, all feel included and important.

Some family members might experience withdrawal from full-time social media, with temporary side effects of fear, loss, anger, anxiety, stress, and maybe a loss of status. Children may argue that they will lose their three hundred friends on Facebook or Twitter. Explain that from among their hundreds of acquaintances, only one or two might be a friend. Teach children that friends come and go, while family will remain steadfast at their side. Patience will assist during the initial days of family time as you stay the course toward individual and family growth.

The rewards can be many, but they're limited by not including all family members, lack of creativity and imagination, or impatience and giving up. Reverse the selfish effects of social media to make family our focused activity away from school and work. Think with your heart and give it your all for months and years of reclaiming quality family time from social media. We deserve better than brief texts, abbreviations, and selfish indulgence.

LIFE'S NOTE 33

A Parent's Best Friend

A dog may be man's best friend, but parents have a new best friend: Khan Academy. If you're familiar with Khan Academy, you already recognize and understand the boost its website can give your intelligence quotient when your child has homework and asks, for example, "What is the relationship of a sine, cosine, and tangent?" If you haven't

> **Question**
>
> Genius knows the resources to teach the answers.

yet discovered Khan Academy, go to khanacademy.org and click on trigonometry. When your kids ask that question, you can introduce them to *soh cah toa*. *Soh* is opposite over hypotenuse, *cah* is adjacent over hypotenuse, and *toa* is opposite over adjacent, which are all relationships of a triangle. You've saved face, and your child thinks you're a genius. Of course, that status lasts only until your child asks, "What are the parts of a human cell?"

Khan Academy is free, world-class online education, with more than 3,800 videos. Its founder, Sal Khan, had a vision of free education available anytime to anyone in the world. He began his quest by converting a closet into a humble office to record educational videos for others to watch and learn at their leisure and watch again as often as necessary. Bill Gates saw Khan Academy's potential and has collaborated with Sal to continually improve and expand it for our benefit and for generations to come.

It may seem like I'm giving Khan Academy free advertising here, but that's not my intent. This a site I've found to be invaluable, one that has the ability to relieve a significant source of tension between parents and children to improve family relationships. I'm happy to be able to introduce others to a useful educational resource.

Each video is approximately nine to ten minutes in length. The videos are simple, with Sal Khan using a virtual blackboard to illustrate concepts. The examples are easy to follow, and Sal's unique voice is comforting and confident. The video format and condensed length appeal to students and are conducive to learning. Students are comfortable with computers and video games, making this a familiar method to maximize learning. Watching the academy's videos is similar, in some ways, to playing a video game. Like a video game, the Khan Academy instructional videos can be viewed repeatedly until the student has the understanding to apply the concept.

This online academy allows students to learn in privacy to avoid embarrassment in the classroom. Customized self-paced learning is the focus to build the student's confidence, allowing kids to achieve their potential and beyond while learning at their own pace. Included is a Knowledge Map for the student to see progress in real time. Khan Academy is a wonder of the world for students of any age to learn skills, from basic arithmetic to calculus, chemistry, physics, computer science, astrology, economics, finance, history, art, and more. For fun, there are recreational mathematics and inspirational videos.

In addition to Khan Academy, parents can use Apples iTunes U and iBooks textbooks for iPad. While Khan Academy is free, Apple has fees for its various offerings. Both offer unique insight and engaging methods to enhance learning and are effective supplements to standard formal education. Let your genius out of the lamp.

LIFE'S NOTE 34

The Fuzzy Wuzzy of Pets

As a youngster, I was allergic to cats and dogs. Allergy medication back then was far less effective than today's assortment of drugs. Small obstacles like this did not prevent my family from having pets, however. We started with a fishbowl of guppies that ate their young. Wow, what a first lesson to learn. Aquatic pets continued with turtles, which were fun. Next were a couple of chickens that, when full-grown, were given to a farmer. Then there was a black and white rabbit named Inky who was cute and soft with a wiggly nose.

While still a youngster and up to today, there have been dogs in my life. I'm so thankful for the companionship and fond memories of dogs named Timber, Candy, and Daisy. When our children were young, we adopted two abandoned newborn rabbits found in the backyard. We housed them in an open box in the kitchen, feeding them stuff rabbits find appealing. Their playground was the kitchen, where they exercised and grew strong. After three months, we released them with ceremony in the backyard. To this day, when I see rabbits in the neighborhood, I think of Chico and Rocket and their ever-growing family tree.

The innocence, devotion, and love from the companionship of pets cannot be denied. Just try it. Adopt a pet and give it a go. You will most likely be surprised by how quickly you fall in love. Of course, pets are not always welcome, for obvious situations like allergies, tenant or subdivision restrictions, discomfort with animals, or unwillingness to have the responsibility of caring for a pet. Though I strongly recommend giving pets a try, those who are coerced into giving in and getting a pet often feel anxiety and resentment that is detrimental to the animal. Pets are not for everyone. Caring for a pet is responsibility that should be enjoyed.

Our most common thought for pets are cats and dogs. But pets come in all forms, shapes, and sizes, with paws and claws, fins and gills, feathers and beaks, shells, slithers and coils, and hoofs and manes. Consider what you like, what fits your personality, the space required, the time needed for loving care, the costs, and the commitment.

We can learn much from the companionship of a pet. Most pets express love and forgiveness without questioning. They are faithful and honest. An owner would be wise to do preliminary research of various breeds and study how to train and understand a pet's behavior before ownership. The training will be less stressful and the rewards magnified.

Stuffed furry animals, books with pictures of animals, and lessons on the sounds of animals are among the first gifts and teachings we do with children. When a young child comes close to a cat or dog, the immediate response is to reach out to touch the fur. The feel of a pet's fur is comforting, as it is similar to that of a child's favorite furry blanket. Children also feel comfortable with pets because here is a creature they can look eye-to-eye or even look down to see. Most pets are creatures who don't appear giant and intimidating. Children now have a new friend or buddy to talk to and play with. Pets offer so many benefits. They nurture wonderment, give a warm need for love, and support parental teaching.

If you have children, a pet is somewhat like having another child. Understand that your children most likely will not help feed, train, or pick up after the pet. If your children do participate with these responsibilities, you are an amazing parent. Children see the pet as their buddy and view parents as the ones who dole out responsibilities and discipline. Pets do none of this parent stuff and have the buddy advantage.

Adults young and old, married or single, also benefit from the joyful companionship of a pet. Pets imitate and in some cases replace the child, giving us an excited welcome greeting at the door after a long day. We can share our fun stories of the day or vent our frustrations, with no fear of judgment or stress. Like a child, we too enjoy hugging a pet to feel the fur and rub the belly. Pets bring out the child in us; we talk to pets the same way we talk to babies, with sayings like, "My cute little pumpkin." It is fun and recalls warm memories of childhood. When old age arrives or our spouse has passed away, pets do their best to fill the void of companionship or quietness. Pets are like shoes—there's a size and color to fit everyone and all ages. Pets are friends, companions, and buddies.

Your Notes

If you were to plan a golden moment, what would it be and how would you do it?

Do you know someone who uses social media in a rude way when in the community of others? If so, would you try to remedy this situation? How?

PART 5

RELATIONSHIPS

How and why we enter into relationships is described in this chapter. Relationships range from acquaintances to friends, marriage, and our relationship with self. Learn how to ask yourself questions to gather information to assess if a relationship is good for you. Consider the suggestions as a way to protect yourself as well as to not waste time and energy. Discover the strength of grounded relationships.

LIFE'S NOTE 35

Identifying When to Commit to Marriage

Marriage is a union of love, with highs and lows much like a ride on a roller coaster. A tip for enjoying the ride is to not get too down when in valleys or too excited riding the peaks. React with moderate levels of emotion for an even keel to smooth the spikes of highs and lows for emotional balanced

> **Advice**
>
> *Saying yes to marriage is an important decision in your life. Be certain of compatibility and joint commitment.*

stability and harmony in a marriage. It is okay to get excited and sad, but following the method of stability and balance will help us to avoid the deep emotional lows and exaggerated jubilation for a marriage of balance and harmony. Furthermore, practice compassion, the art of compromise, and forgiveness for life and marriage to be filled with joy and enthusiastic, enduring love. Entering into marriage is a commitment of partnership until death do you part.

Do you have what it takes? The answer to that question must be an unequivocal *yes* before you consider joining hands in the union of marriage. A commonly repeated statistic is that 50 percent of marriages will end in divorce, and whether or not that's actually accurate, we certainly have all seen or experienced in our own lives marriages that didn't survive or shouldn't have been entered into in the first place. Will we marry with our glass half-empty or half-full? Are we pessimists or optimists about our marriage lasting throughout our lifetime? The odds seem similar to a coin flip. Are we willing to stake the success of our marriage on the outcome of a coin flip? Doing so would be ridiculous. Then why do some of us spend less effort evaluating and soul-searching to decide on a future spouse than we do deciding on which house or car to purchase?

Take time and be patient. Do the research for a thorough review of the potential success and longevity of your marriage as well as your happiness. Honesty with your assessment comes from not only thinking with your heart but also with your mind and soul. All three must be in agreement before you consider this person as your spouse. If any of the three are not in agreement, do not try to rationalize. Instead, accept your assessment and move on rather than make a drastic mistake.

Considering a future partner will have you facing many questions, making either wise or misguided conclusions to either marry this person or to say no. The following is a comprehensive checklist for help in making a well-thought-out decision.

Wise Conclusions	*Misguided Conclusions*

I am getting married . . .

because we love one another.	because I want companionship.
because we want a family to nurture.	because I want to have a child.
because we want to support and care for each other.	just to settle down.
for monogamy.	for a sexual companion.
with an attitude of *we* and *us*.	with an attitude of *I* and *me*.
for acceptance.	for appearances.
for two-way romance and love.	because how I feel is all that's important.
to share my life with another.	to be with another.
to fulfill both of our needs and dreams.	to save, help, or change my spouse.
to have a connection with another to love and grow emotionally.	because my friends are getting married.
because I definitely love this person.	because I can't be with someone else.
because I expect more.	because this my only chance.
because we want to be with each other and we took our time to decide.	because I'm tired of being single.
	because I was pressured to marry.
because I'm ready to make a commitment.	because we've lived together long enough.

for the love in our relationship.	for the love of money.
because I believe in myself.	because I need security.
to have a loving family.	because we're pregnant.
out of natural love.	out of forced love.

A prenuptial agreement is like an insurance policy, and it contradicts the spirit of marriage. It seems to be a selfish approach to protect material wealth. The future spouse being asked to sign trades freedom for a relationship of control. Be wary of swapping your soul for materialistic gain and hollow happiness. If you sign a prenuptial agreement with the selfish intent of financial comfort, you are likely marrying for the wrong reasons and will be lonely and unhappy.

Living together is a convenient way out for those who fear commitment. Getting married because of a pregnancy, though admirable and in many cases good for the child, will demand more effort to follow life's elements of goodness for the marriage to endure. Based on what I've heard and read from others, it seems that getting married young, a few years out of high school, increases the odds of a marriage dissolving. Take your time to get to know the good and questionable characteristics of a person before considering marriage.

Consider these other concerns for successful and enduring marriages:

- *Communication* must be two-way, including listening.
- *Trust* comes from honesty and integrity.
- *Goals*, shared and individual, should be something spouses work together to achieve.
- *Moral values* and ideas of goodness should be shared.
- *Spirituality* should be compatible.
- *Different political attitudes* could divide couples.
- *Alcohol consumption*—quantity, effect on personality, and costs to quality of life—is a concern that should not be underestimated.
- *Smoking* also causes major problems, including health impairments, annoyance, odor, effect on intimacy, and costs to quality of life.
- *Abusive behavior and language* cannot be ignored; watch out for signs.
- *Sexual compatibility* is important to the health of a marriage.

- *Emotional support*, heartfelt consideration, and kindness should run both ways.
- *Education* can be an issue if the spouses are not at similar levels.
- *The past*, if it was challenging and difficult, can be hard for spouses to rise above.
- *Fear of failure* can cause apprehension and a self-fulfilling prophesy of a marriage that fails.
- *Fear that marriage is forever* can also be a concern, causing lack of commitment that sabotages the marriage.
- *Compatible income level* is helpful so that the spouses have one accustomed lifestyle. If not, doubt and resentment may spring up.

If you feel overwhelmed by all of these factors to consider before marrying, take a deep breath and slow down, as most factors will surface and be easily recognizable with little or no effort on our part. Privately recording our findings helps us do a comprehensive and thorough assessment to make decisions in our best interests and the best interests of our potential spouse. Deciding on a spouse is one of the most important and impactful decisions we make in the course of our life and for our quality of life.

Marrying for the right reasons begins, as is said in movie trailers, an epic adventure. Our journey and adventure will require work and commitment from both spouses for a happy and enduring marriage. Marriage is a partnership of *we* and *us*, instead of *I* and *me*. Throw in pinches of curious spontaneity for romance, variety, and freshness. Follow life's elements of goodness, and you will do just fine. Whether you decide to marry or live solo, enjoy the adventurous ride. Wish everyone the best and the most out of life.

Me? I'm celebrating thirty-eight years of marriage and counting.

LIFE'S NOTE 36

Building an Enduring Marriage

In this note, *enduring* means "until death do us part." Marriages that endure share common threads of supporting each other through tough times and times of joy. The journey of marriage is a roller-coaster ride with peaks and valleys of excitement and emotional challenge. Before asking for another's hand and throughout the time of blissful engagement, discuss the sentiments of marriage to establish and foster honest two-way communication.

> ### Advice
>
> *Hope your marriage is a long, enjoyable, and memorable ride. Love and appreciation make the ride worthwhile.*

Communication is the foundation for all other common threads of healthy marriages. Navigating through challenging times with grounded communication solidifies the bond of marriage and preserves bubbly love for one another. Cherish heartfelt giddy feelings for your spouse and your marriage. Communication is simply sharing thoughts and feelings, coupled with compassionate listening free of judgment.

Compromise within marriage contributes to respectful communication without the risk of division. When you address issues or problems that create conflict, consider varying suggestions, and think with your heart and the heart of your spouse, you can work toward a solution of compromise to subdue conflict. Marriages in which the spouses think only of *I* and *me* are susceptible to stress and likely to contain conflict with no healthy resolution. The partnership of marriage is better served when both spouses share an attitude of *we* and *us* and make compromises to preserve and strengthen the bond of marriage.

Forgiveness must be a staple for marriage to flourish. Though the act of forgiving may be difficult, we should be able to understand the "why" of forgiveness. How to forgive is the difficult part, as we are unsure of what to do and may be unwilling to do it. There is no perfect proven method to express forgiveness with heartfelt intent; just be truthful, honest, and genuine. If you are the one being forgiven, accept forgiveness, as tough as it may seem, and move on from this hurdle rather than carrying baggage of resentment and bitterness. Forgiveness is critical to restoring, preserving, and strengthening our partnership, and for our marriage to flourish and last. Forgiveness is freedom.

Respect requires us to continually practice communication, compromise, and forgiveness. These are the three legs that support a marriage. When any one of the three is weakened or missing, the marriage tilts or collapses, requiring immediate attention. Determine which leg or legs needs attention to balance and restore marital harmony.

Commitment starts in our heart and endures from our soul. Have patience to learn to adapt and adjust, with resiliency to achieve the satisfaction of shared happiness and a tight bond of enduring marriage. Commitment means to never consider giving in or giving up, and working through rumbling emotions to preserve a marriage.

Passion is easily lost in a marriage because of interfering career demands and challenges as well as the hustle and bustle of family responsibilities. Find even tiny moments to express affection and appreciation for each other. A wink, smile, hug, kiss, tender touch, fond light pat, or whisper of love all resonate with appreciation and gratitude for our spouse. We all like to feel the recognition of affection and appreciation to acknowledge our commitment and love for each other. Passion is the flame.

Romance's light begs for fuel to shine bright rather than flicker intermittently. Once the knot of marriage is tied, the romance of dating and engagement need not go away. Instead, intensify the romance to keep marriage fresh, new, and warm. Reignite the passion for each other with sparks of romance to kindle the fire inside, helping it to burn hot and long. Romance can be found in acts of kindness, such as tender words, candlelight dinners, loving care, surprises, unexpected gifts, snuggling, whispers of love, and dates sharing mutual interests or—better yet—the interests of our spouse and those of our imagination. Let the light of romance burn bright and never go out, continuing to gently melt the wax.

Spontaneity brings risk and danger for exciting times to explore and discover each other. When your spouse offers a spontaneous idea, consider dropping what you're doing, as your spouse thought of this idea on the spur of the moment to share this time with you. Do not underestimate the impact of spontaneity for an enthusiastic, passionate, romantic marriage.

Bring out the kid in you. Children know how to play, laugh, and be silly. If you have forgotten or think you are above acting childlike, observe the joy and innocence of children to laugh and be bubbly. Inject some kid behavior into your marriage for silliness to nurture the positive effects of humor, joy, and laughter. Maybe spray your spouse with silly string, jump out to scare him or her, play games, go to a park, make faces, or follow your own silly ideas. Of course these are silly. However, they never get old or dull. Invite smiles and laughter into your marriage with good old-fashioned childlike silliness.

Consider all the above for love to continue to permeate your marriage. Express love for your spouse frequently with heartfelt gestures and whispers. A whisper of love echoes loudly. An early morning expression of affection resonates throughout the day, embracing your spouse with warmth and appreciation. Love offers gratitude for the contributions and commitment of your spouse. Love often, love loud, and love long. Love your marriage and celebrate it.

Pillars for an Enduring Marriage

- communication
- compromise
- forgiveness
- respect
- commitment
- passion
- romance
- spontaneity
- childlike silliness

LIFE'S NOTE 37

Living Solo

Social change continues to accelerate, with a plethora of external factors influencing the evolution of how we live and socialize. More Americans are living alone than ever before as a result of being divorced, widowed, or choosing to stay single. In "Nine Myths About Living Alone," a 2012 article on the AARP website at aarp.org, writer Wendy Smith cites some big changes in who and how many people choose to live alone these days. Some statistics:

> **Inspiration**
>
> *Living solo is to be the composer and musician to write and play the music of each day.*

- While only 4 million American adults lived alone in 1950, that number is now up to 31 million, more than 50 percent of adults in the US.
- In 1950, single adults made up 9 percent of US households; today, it's 28 percent.
- Adults age eighteen to thirty-four are choosing to be single in greater numbers than ever, at 5 million now over 500,000 in 1950.

Many factors can lead to the decision to live solo: divorce, death, desire for freedom, finances, independence, broken relationships, or other personal reasons. Be realistic with your expectations for living solo, knowing that utopia is as unlikely here as it can be in marriage. However, a place of comfort and peaceful solitude is certainly realistic and obtainable. Some people want to be free from acceptance by others, constant companionship, as well as emotional rifts of live-in relationships. Some say they prefer living alone and are not interested in marriage. Others seem happier after getting out of an unhappy marriage and are in no rush to get married again.

Neither marriage nor living solo assures happiness or bliss. Living solo requires us to be comfortable in our own skin and accept ourselves for who we are as we are. To be comfortable, we need to accept our appearance and who we are inside. If we are not completely comfortable with ourselves, living solo offers the solitude for self-discovery free of critique and criticism.

Sometimes loneliness can be an issue causing stress in either a marriage or living single. To address or prevent loneliness, surround yourself with family and friends, and do things you enjoy to energize yourself. Lean on your network of friends to socialize and do fun stuff with to further appreciate their friendship. Some degree of feeling connected is important when loneliness surfaces. Your best prescription for erasing loneliness is to get together with friends to socialize. If you have a poor family relationship, friends can provide the feeling of family and belonging. Lack of interaction can lead to or prolong loneliness and depression. People living alone are encouraged to have active social relationships with family and friends, and to take plenty of pictures with family and friends as a reminder of that connectedness.

Continually add to your social network by creating opportunities to make friends. Join a club or organization, or volunteer to support a favorite cause. Participation in groups reinforces a sense of belonging as well as meaning and purpose for your well-being. Find what brings you enjoyment and satisfaction. Maybe it's a hobby, music, dancing, movies, sports, or reading. Treat yourself to the finest electronics and gadgets to fully enjoy your interests. Marvel at your accomplishments. Sing loud and often. Dance crazy with a smile. Eat and drink all you want while watching a movie. Scream and yell as a fan should for your favorite sports team. Get on the field, course, or path, or dive in the pool, and be an athlete. Read voraciously to learn and discover. You are in control. Celebrate life.

An earlier note discussed the benefits of having a pet, and they're particularly of value to people living alone. Of course, there's also responsibility and time required to care for and love a pet. The minor inconveniences of caring for a pet are outweighed for most people by the love and companionship only a pet can offer. Pets are unassuming, nonjudgmental, and great listeners. Imagine a dog greeting you at the door with a wagging tail and loving eyes, or a cat rubbing against you and jumping in your lap to be close and loved. You can share anything with a pet; it won't care what you say but will listen for hours free of criticism and judgment. Therapeutic conversation like this releases stress and initiates a fresh perspective to see that what was once perceived as a problem is instead a minor nuisance not worthy of further attention.

Whether we live single or with others, we can decorate the interior of our place to match our personality or enhance it. If tranquility fits your personality, consider the Asian minimalist Zen-like approach of harmony, balance, and order. Maybe you are bold and excitable. If so, design a cave or a tailgating atmosphere. Wanting to look and feel your best, design with the catered and pampered style of a hotel, winery, or spa motif. No matter your style, make your place your own to get energy and happiness flowing into your days.

Reasons for Choosing to Live Solo

- You're the boss of you.
- You have freedom of choice.
- You answer only to yourself.
- You can be self-sufficient.
- You feel happier on your own.
- You enjoy peace and quiet.
- You need a place and time to recharge.
- You risk incompatibility with roommates.
- You don't want to deal with irritating habits or idiosyncrasies.
- You're free from criticism and judgment.
- You're free of intolerance.
- You're free of distractions.
- If you make a mistake, no one else knows or cares.
- Living alone is more comfortable for you.
- You're on a journey of self-discovery.
- Being independent boosts your confidence and self-esteem.
- You feel a sense of empowerment when living alone.

Reasons to Have a Roommate

- You're susceptible to loneliness and depression.
- You want to save money by sharing expenses.
- You want someone to share household duties.

- You're afraid of feeling lonely.
- Living alone is boring.
- You want diversity in your life.
- You enjoy having someone to talk to and share stories.
- You want to feel connected.

Living solo as the result of a divorce is a challenge, with emotions of loss, betrayal, trust, and not feeling loved along with other factors wearing at your balance and well-being. Suddenly and unexpectedly needing to live single is a shock, with little time for transition. This challenge is thrown in your lap with no direction and with the fear and uncertainty of the unknown. Having been accustomed to an environment of social interaction and now being in a position with limited interaction darkens your days with loneliness and confusing, chaotic emotions.

Surround yourself with supportive family and friends to attempt to establish a new normalcy. Stay connected with this support group as often as possible for belief, faith, and hope that you will emerge okay and, depending upon the circumstances, as a healthier and stronger person. Be patient, persevere, and overcome the challenges of divorce to move on for your well-being. With the support of others, you can and will succeed.

It is sad to say that widows and widowers come in all ages. Life is going along great with peace, happiness, and appreciation, and then unexpectedly a traumatic event or illness takes away your beloved partner. Having shared a few years or decades of joy and laughter along with trials and tribulations only increases the feeling of loss and emptiness. The unknown is unnerving and scary. Combine these feelings with old age, limited mobility, and the income challenges of living solo and the stress, loneliness, and worry are magnified.

Imagine being a younger person losing a partner and having to care for young children and work, with all the responsibility now resting on your shoulders. Living as a solo adult and parent in today's quick-to-judge society is particularly challenging, as others scrutinize your every decision and move. Forget about the self-serving gossip to focus and concentrate on yourself and your children. First take care of yourself, so that you have the strength to care for your children. Use family and friends as your support group to help you maintain a sense of balance and well-being. Don't be shy about asking family and friends for help to share in the responsibilities. Find your positives and all the goodness around and within you for the appreciation and gratitude to celebrate one day at a time. At a time like this, gratitude might be difficult to find, but rest assured the positives are there. With the passing of time, the positives and goodness will nurture your balance and well-being.

If you're alone by choice or by circumstance, please don't rely on social media as your sole source of communication and social interaction. Replace texting with cordial phone calls to talk live, and get together face-to-face to interact and benefit from smiles, warm eyes, and hugs. Network to develop a core group of friends—your go-to friends. Start a "living solo" group to connect through social events to share fun, laughter, and smiles. Living solo does not necessarily mean living single. Be active.

Inspiration

Appreciate the solitude and calmness to see the beauty and celebrate each day.

LIFE'S NOTE 38

Circle of Friends

Healthy relationships are paramount for our well-being from childhood to old age. Today's economic and social dynamics require relocation, and few friends last an entire lifetime. Most often, they come and go. A warm, outgoing personality and the skill to establish friendships will serve you well. As relocation and other factors strain relationships, embrace your core friends to preserve and grow friendships as you strive to add to your list of friends.

> **Tip**
>
> *True friends stay in our circle when times get tough.*

Telling an acquaintance from a friend can easily be clouded by a desire for close relationships. Your enthusiasm to add a friend to your list may be overly generous. For assistance, consider these defining points of a friend: someone you know well and who knows you, cares for you, and supports you; someone who is loyal and trustworthy; and someone who stays in your circle in time of need. Like family, friends are there when work needs to be done as well as for the fun stuff.

Finding friends takes work. An isolated single life restricts opportunities to meet candidates for friendship. Place yourself in situations where people gather to increase your pool of possible friendships. Be outgoing and introduce yourself without making a big deal of it. Follow the proven method of asking questions to get others to talk about themselves and then genuinely listen. People like to tell their story. Ideally, there will be some give and take, some listening and sharing, as you get to know each other. Remain patient and allow the relationship to develop from an acquaintance to a friendship.

Abusing the convenience and comfort of a friendship will most likely stress the relationship or end it. Expecting too much from a friend also creates strain. Foster a relaxed atmosphere free of criticism, confrontation, and expectations. Support your friends, expecting nothing in return. Ignore idiosyncrasies, as they don't truly matter. Accept your friends as they are.

Friendship is a two-way street. Drive more in the lane of giving instead of taking for the friendship to endure. If in the past you had a friend move away or become distant, you tend to become reluctant to give so much in the future for fear of losing a friend and feeling hurt. Fear and skepticism invite isolation, hindering your ability to move forward. Review past friendships to determine if maybe your willingness to give so much was interpreted as overbearing. It is not so much how often you give, but more your quality of giving.

Qualities of a Friend

- loyal
- ally
- helpful
- trustworthy
- giving
- supportive
- cares about you

LIFE'S NOTE 39

Communication: Social Media and the Real World

Decades ago, communication was simpler, with face-to-face contact, phone calls, mail, and telegrams as the only options. A telegram was abbreviated like a tweet but sent through a phone line to a telegraph office where we physically picked it up or

had it delivered to our door. Today, communication is far more broad and complex. Pagers, fax machines (the early pioneers), computers, notebooks, and smart phones combined with the vastness of the Internet and social media have altered the landscape of social communication and how we communicate. It seems we spend far too much time in the virtual world.

Basic skills of speaking and listening are being challenged by the shortened length of online and text messages as well as our need to abbreviate words. Virtual and live, in-person communication are both so ingrained in societal structure that the two must meld to complement both acquaintance- and relationship-based communication.

The world of virtual communication is quick with comments and ideas, and responses are expected within an equally shortened window of time. Speed is both a strength and a weakness of social media, as well as a yellow light of caution. This need for expected speed weakens our ability to speak fully formed thoughts face to face and diminishes our communication skills and the importance of listening. Preservation of meaningful conversation and genuine listening must be a focus for us and generations to come to both nurture new relationships and deepen the bond of relationships in progress.

Rather than prefer one format of communication over another, compare the two to better understand the value of each. Some of the differences are obvious, whereas others are subtle. With an open mind, we can learn the contribution and importance of both to meld them for effective relationship-oriented communication.

Social Media	*Live, In-Person*
Miss people's reactions and body language	See people's reactions and body language
More open to misinterpretation	Better understanding from closeness
Time to think	Less time to respond and improve skills
Safe from emotions	Emotional integration
More control	More open to judgment
Hidden presence	Vulnerability of appearance and gesture
Spontaneity—risky	
Correct mistakes before sending	Mistakes more apparent
More relaxed	Fear of failure
Less sense of responsibility	Listen (if only from accountability to respond)
Thought through and measured	

Most of us have learned from our spontaneity and clumsy awkwardness at fast-paced virtual-world communication not to click send too quickly. Practice the skills of speaking and listening to be effective and responsible with both virtual and real-world communication. Another conduit for learning and honing communication skills continues to be what some consider the old-fashioned method of live and in-person face-to-face communication and public speaking. Practicing these two methods will assist in fostering communication skills with acquaintances, friends, and those to whom we are deeply bonded. Normally we have more acquaintances than friends and fewer deeply bonded relationships than the other two. Understand the difference to better plan and invest your time wisely and for your future.

LIFE'S NOTE 40

Character of Conversation

Forms of conversation range from nonthreatening idle chatter to gossip and intellectual, purposeful, goal-oriented discussion. How we converse to express our thoughts and opinions reflects our personality. Our communication style reflects our conversational skills,

> **Tip**
>
> More is learned from listening. Listening is hindered by too many people talking.

confidence, willingness to take a risk, and comfort with vulnerability. Most often our conversation is a blend of a few forms. Conversation is an art form, with one form or style usually dominating and identifying our character.

Neutral talk is the most common form of expression when meeting an acquaintance or friend with little time or desire to invest. Brief talk like this has limited interest and lacks genuine care. We choose this method to be free of any risk or vulnerability. Commonly used expressions are "How are you?" "What's up?" and "What's going on?"; the usual response is "Good" or "Fine," "Not much," or "Same old same old." It lacks follow-up to generate further dialogue. Neutral talk is more of a generic greeting than a conversation.

Small talk slightly increases the dialogue with some variety. Some popular introductory comments with small talk refer to the weather, local or national news, sports, or reality shows to break the ice. We begin to listen more intently and show more interest. Personal thoughts and opinions are now expressed, introducing some risk with minimal vulnerability limited by the topics discussed. Small talk and neutral talk remain free of care and true interest in the other person.

Relationship talk introduces a higher level of risk and vulnerability from expressing genuine care and emotional interest in another person. Questions become more complicated, with answers involving feelings and emotions. Initially, we remain protective of the vulnerability of our inner self, resisting exposure and the accompanying risks of harming the relationship. Now both risk and vulnerability are magnified, but so too are the rewards. Be patient, respectful, and at times forgiving to nurture the relationship to bloom into deeper a connection.

Intellectual conversation has vision and explores ideas to develop plans and strategies to reach solutions. This is discussion of implied order and respect for others' thoughts and opinions. We feed off one another to ignite deeper thought and initiate creative ideas for a call to action.

Then there is *gossip*, which is defined as idle chatter about others. With neutral talk, the engine is quiet, whereas with gossip, the engine is racing with talk in overdrive, accompanied with minimal listening. Gossip is a self-centered, pat-on-the-back, did-you-know, weak one-way attempt at conversation. It's like a tabloid focusing on trials, tribulations, and misfortunes. We do this at the expense—and sometimes the embarrassment—of others. Engaging in gossip shows a lack of care, compassion, and respect for others. Practicing gossip carries with it expressions of sharp criticism, throwing someone under the bus, or stabbing someone in the back. Why do some of us choose to gossip? Reasons include lack of confidence, poor conversation skills, inability to contribute value, or the need to be the first to share "breaking news." Participating in gossip exposes our weaknesses and our desire to speak poorly of others. Think of how others will perceive you if you gossip. They might see you as a tabloid reporter or one needing the assistance of a megaphone to be heard. How sad.

Conversation requires the skills of speaking and, more importantly, listening. You need to listen intently with care and compassion to understand what another is saying. Avoid trying to read between the lines. If you are unsure of the other person's words, ask questions to be clear and avoid misunderstandings. Compassionate conversation consists of feelings and sharing of private emotions, requiring those listening to have empathy to relate to the other's position so as to contribute comforting, supportive thoughts.

Not only is conversation a skill, it is also an art form to continually hone to respect the thoughts, feelings, and privacy of others, in consideration for their well-being and ours.

Your Notes

What are the strengths and weaknesses of your potential spouse?

What are you doing to ensure that your marriage endures?

List two friends and what they mean to you.

PART 6

How we feel at any given time is based on our emotions. Emotions range from neutral to chaotic and debilitating. Learn how to release and manage your emotions rather than letting your emotions manage you.

LIFE'S NOTE 41

Transform Grief

Today my mother, our children's grandmother and our grandson's great grandmother, passed away. This is a note of appreciation and gratitude that has lived in my heart forever. Mom will be missed. She continued to teach and inspire me through the process of dying. She was at peace and calm, knowing she had limited time.

> **Tip**
>
> *Beauty in grieving the loss of a loved one shines from the remembrance of many golden moments.*

Death need not be frightening or ugly. Given notice, the process of dying and eventual passing away can be a calming time with awareness of our fragility as well as our resiliency and our capacity for love and compassion. Through this experience, we learn from our loved ones the lessons of life.

We learn that we do not have full control, if any, of the amount of time we have on earth. What we do have is the freedom to choose to make the most of our time. Family should be the focus of our remaining days. The family bond is unlike any other, with ties running deep, touching our heart and soul with goodness and love forever. Friends can come and go. Families endure.

Family members understandably want to prolong the days of a loved one. In some cases, this is understandable. It can be extremely difficult to put the feelings and wishes of a loved one before our own feelings. But if our loved ones are at peace and feel their life is fulfilled, their work is done, and they are prepared for life everlasting, it seems selfish to want to extend life and deny our loved one a place of spiritual peace and serenity. Being unselfish and respectful are lessons that we are taught early and continue to be taught in the waning years and hours before passing away. It was my mother's time, and it was beautiful. A loved one's life is to be remembered and celebrated.

Mom will continue her life from afar forever, teaching her family further lessons for a life filled with love, meaning, and purpose. Her hand will be on our shoulders, touching and holding us through times of joy, sadness, and deliberation. She will continue to remind us of her teachings of love, compassion, and forgiveness. For that, we are forever grateful.

Mom, you will be missed but never forgotten. There is now a void that will echo your love and memories for the rest of time. You will live on. You did your work with patience, perseverance, love, compassion, and commitment, with a gold medal around your neck and resting over your heart. Thank you for having such high standards, and for your unselfishness in putting all others before yourself. You are proof that there are angels and saints among us.

LIFE'S NOTE 42

Stress Management

Stress-inducing conditions and situations surround us each and every day. Being oblivious to the signs of stress and its effects on emotional and physical health is detrimental to your daily well-being and balance. Stress gnawing at your psyche, left unchecked, conditions you

to accept stress as a daily part of life. You are responsible and have the choice to take control to manage stress.

Sheltering yourself with a shield to completely avoid stressful situations is living life in fear and risk-avoidance. Wishing to be stress-free is nice but not realistic. Too many potential stressors exist for us to achieve immunity from stress. Stress affects us all with varying degrees of severity. Strive to incorporate the basic fundamentals for stress management.

Take ownership over stress. You are the driver of how you choose to live your life. Drivers are not idle passengers. Drivers are in control to actively navigate up and over challenges like stress. Be free from the fog of stress clouding your vision to clearly see the road and arrive at your destination of managing stress to remain in control.

Signs of stress come in numerous forms, from subtle to obvious. Stress skews our perspective, gradually migrating it from optimism to pessimism. There is a definite change in attitude from positivity to negativity. Compassion is no longer a strength, instead leading us to quick, thoughtless judgment. Days are filled with anxiety. Anger raises its ugly face instead of mild dislike or disagreement. Thoughts of bitterness, envy, and pity begin to surface. We become aggressive and unwilling to compromise. Sleepless nights or less sleep reduce our ability to function. Eating for the sake of eating or gaining weight is a telltale sign. These and more are red flags waving us down to address what could be debilitating stress and, if left unchecked, depression.

Congratulations—you have recognized the signs and concluded there is measurable stress in your life requiring attention. Take a deep breath to slow down so as not to panic or feel overwhelmed. Rest assured there are steps to initiate a plan to feel in control with hope to manage your stress.

Take ownership over stress instead of letting it own you. Thoughts create emotions. You need a method to control your thoughts, and patience and persistence are the building blocks for managing stress and sustaining well-being. Follow this method of win/win. Your first win comes from acknowledging your stress. Begin immediately by recording on paper your stressors and how they affect you.

Sometimes you hold on to stressors to use as excuses or accept as your normal way of life. An exercise to erase this restrictive type of thought is to closely review each stressor to honestly evaluate its level of negative impact on your psyche. Rate them one to five, with five being the most severe. Those rated a one or maybe a two are more than likely nuisance stressors that you can let go of and forget about. This exercise establishes a sense of control to begin to understand the dynamics of stress. Use this journal as your starting or base point to measure progress or regression.

Learn to control your environment and commit to memory a cache of tips to address stress and stressful situations. Responding to times of stress by immediately ignoring the situation is something we believe defuses or minimizes its effects. Unfortunately, we have done nothing to improve our situation. We have procrastinated to delay facing our stressors. Reacting with indifference inhibits our ability to act responsibly to control and conquer stressful situations. Inaction also sets the tone for procrastination, hoping the situation will magically pass without effort. This approach exacerbates and prolongs the control stress has over us. Act now.

Tips to Manage and Control Stress

- Do not worry or be concerned with things beyond your control.
- Determine whether the stress comes from a genuine source or is self-induced.
- Avoid situations known to be stressful.
- Learn to say no. Don't try to be all things to all people.

- Avoid overanalyzing or reading between the lines.
- Don't be quick to judge. Instead, show compassion.
- Be willing to compromise.
- Discover the freedom of forgiveness.
- Avoid provocative and sensitive topics, such as politics and religion.
- Cease trying to be perfect. Your expectations are unrealistic.
- Get away from thinking that every minute must count and be productive.
- Set time aside for yourself.
- Learn to relax. Free yourself from constant scheduling.
- Have time for fun and silliness to reset your attitude.
- Celebrate positive times and progress.
- Have an attitude of optimism and positivity.
- Have the perspective to look at problems as opportunities to learn and grow.
- Exercise.
- Eat healthy.
- Get the proper amount of sleep. Most of us need more.
- Avoid the crutch of alcohol and drugs to mask the stress or you'll never be free.
- Record in your journal how you feel when faced with a stressful situation, what you believe caused you to be stressed, and what you did to defuse the stress.
- Talk it through.
- Seek professional help if necessary.

Skills to Manage and Control Stress

- Recognize stressors.
- Be assertive to take control.
- Assess the effect stressors have on you and how they make you feel.
- Formulate a plan to beat your stress.
- Commit to memory tips to defuse and minimize stress in your life.
- Be realistic that there will always be some form of stress.

- Differentiate between stressful stress and nuisance stress.
- Keep a journal to map your progress or alter your course.
- Follow your heart to discover what truly matters in life. Recall the list of tips during stressful situations to walk away from stress and realize that it may actually be no big deal.
- Don't be your own worst enemy. Chill out, relax, and be less sensitive to get away from living on the edge of stress.

Have faith to believe in yourself and do not give up. It takes less energy to manage stress than to live with it.

LIFE'S NOTE 43

It's Okay to Cry

Plenty of conditions and situations bring on tears. Sometimes the hurt is so deep from the pain of physical, verbal, or emotional abuse that we cry. Of course crying will occur from any situation causing mistrust and lack of respect to hurt so deep to feel unappreciated and unloved. In this case, we often use crying as a survival mechanism. If this is how you're trying to survive, please look for a change of environment, as no one deserves or should suffer through such pain.

Yes, it is okay to cry. There are many things that influence or touch us in such a way that crying happens naturally. Sometimes it catches us off guard when we don't want others to see us crying. Pictures, movies, books, pets, the beauty of a child or grandchild, sound, touch, fragrance, and spoken words are just some of the things that cause us to cry.

> **Inspiration**
>
> *Crying washes away emotions to see the rainbow through the tears.*

Crying can be an indication of a warm, giving, loving, and sentimental heart. Be grateful your heart can be touched so deeply that your eyes water and tears flow down your cheeks. Sometimes we try to prevent that first tear from falling by wiping our eyes, as we are embarrassed to have others see us crying and sense our weakness. If your heart is touched so deeply that you cry, how is this weakness? Let the tears fall. Give thanks and be grateful for having a caring heart.

Maybe you see no value or only weakness in crying, and that's okay. However, you could be missing opportunities for higher consciousness of all the good surrounding you and within you. Crying, even if only once and privately, could be the point where change occurs for deeper love and compassion. This is not to say you are a bad person. It is to say that you might improve or feel better from a cry.

What are the possible ramifications of not crying? Stress continues to build and you miss a way to release some tension. Crying is similar to boiling water in a coffeepot. When the pot has more pressure than it can handle, the valve on top releases pressure to maintain balance inside. Crying is your valve to release pressure and achieve balance. By choosing not to cry, you miss signals from within to explore who you really are. You miss discovering bits and pieces connecting your heart, soul, and mind for purposeful well-being. Keeping from crying also impedes your appreciation and gratitude for the lessons learned and the experiences and challenges faced leading you to where you are today.

Various types of crying happen throughout life. Let's examine a few of the reasons we cry.

- *Joy*: This is usually referred to as a good cry. We are so moved with joy that we cry.
- *Sadness*: We become overwhelmed with emotion as our lips quiver, our heart beats slightly faster, and we become warm and so unhappy that we cry.
- *Grief*: A jarring and tiring cry comes out of love, compassion, and loss. Emotional pain is real and engraved by a deep emotional bond. Yes, this is a good cry in a manner of love, respect, admiration, and gratitude for a life shared.
- *Emotions*: Some crying can result from the end of a relationship, hurtful words, or ridicule; feeling ignored or unappreciated; bullying, and too many other emotional experiences to mention. This is a severe, hurtful type of pain that induces crying.
- *Stress*: Usually, stress is a result of conditions, situations, or pressures overwhelming us to feel pinned in a corner with no way out. In this situation, crying can be a stress reliever. The relief may last only so long. But yes, this can be a good cry.
- *Beauty*: We might cry from the beauty of a child, spouse, parent, relationship, friendship, pet, animal, Mother Nature, the sky, a loving memory, a special holiday, and much more. The hope is this is our longest list of reasons we cry.

LIFE'S NOTE 44

Self-Esteem Is Your Opinion of Yourself

L ow self-esteem is easily recognizable from the self-doubt and lack of self-confidence that go along with it. Lack of belief in yourself begins to sour your relationships and career. Below are the telltale signs of low self-esteem:

- lack of self-confidence
- self-doubt
- reserved manner
- questioning self
- passivity—lack of quality contributions to situations
- easily influenced by peer pressure
- easily influenced by others' words and actions
- negativity
- trouble socializing
- change in academic focus
- unusual time alone
- posture—slouching, looking down or away

Advice

Don't settle for half of you. Discover and appreciate it all.

High self-esteem is primarily characterized by the presence of confidence and self-worth. We are proud and accept who we are and our appearance. There exists a belief and faith that we are good, with much to offer. High self-esteem reinforces and gives us the confidence to face challenges and deal with life's distractions for far better outcomes. Problems are now perceived as opportunities to learn and grow. Our interactions with others are more positive and enthusiastic. We respect ourselves and are confident in our social life, nurturing healthy relationships and our own well-being. The chart that follows shows how high and low self-esteem differ.

Low Self-Esteem	High Self-Esteem
Poor opinion of self	Comfortable with self
Doubt in self	Confident
Lack of self-worth and value	Presence of self-worth and value
Excessively passive	Proud
Lack of confidence	Self-accepting
Succumbing to peer pressure	Respecting who you are
Influenced by others	Inspiring to self and others
Reserved	Taking appropriate action
Negative	Positive
Pessimistic	Optimistic
Lazy	Energetic

Outside influences are usually the cause of low self-esteem. Understand that poor self-esteem was not caused by you. You are not a bad person. You have gifts waiting to be awakened when you appreciate your self-worth. Believe in yourself.

Points to Improve Self-Esteem

- Replace insecurity and doubt with belief in yourself.
- Surround yourself with positivity.
- Set realistic expectations—they must be obtainable. Start slowly and then gradually heighten your expectations.
- Learn to think with your heart instead of your mind to modify your thinking away from conflict, doubt, and confusion toward a loving, compassionate diet of goodness.
- View mistakes as opportunities, not failures. Replace the fear of failure with perspective to learn for progress and growth.
- Take pride in contributions; they add value to a situation or idea.
- Be adventurous. Try new things to expand your horizons and comfort zone. Being stuck in a rut clouds vision for self-discovery.

- Have "Fundays"—planned days of fun and silliness to laugh and celebrate. (See Note 62 for more on what makes a Funday.)
- Take ownership of your self-worth and self-esteem. What is your opinion of yourself?

LIFE'S NOTE 45

The Ups and Downs of Attitude

Volumes have been written about the effects of a positive attitude and positive thinking. The principle is quite simple and similar to that for computers: garbage in, garbage out. Good stuff in, good stuff out. If we surround ourselves with negativity and pessimism, what should we expect? Do not be surprised if your days are duds filled with negative emotions and pity. Ultimately we control our attitude, not others. People will try to influence our attitude. If

> **Tip**
>
> Being so into ourselves keeps others away.

their influence is negative, disassociate yourself and seek out supporting, positive people.

Continuing to allow a negative environment to rot your attitude speaks of poor self-esteem, self-pity, and giving in. Realistically, it can be extremely difficult to completely change or influence your environment because of circumstances of age, dependency, and fear of peer pressure. If this sounds or feels familiar, understand that there is a way to begin to escape this influence of negativity. Immerse yourself in secondary environments where there is positive support and encouragement. Look to church, school, family, relatives, friends, sports, music, or whatever else fills you with positive energy. Conjure up the strength to say "No more, I've had enough." You deserve better and should expect more for yourself.

It is easy to say, "Make it happen." It is not so easy to actually make it happen. Positive thinking is a start. Begin by perceiving situations from a positive perspective. Instead of seeing a problem, see an opportunity; get off the train of pessimism to jump aboard the train of optimism. See your glass as half-full, and fill it up with positivity. Negative people see their glass as half-empty and are attracted to other negative thinkers. Positivity will either alter others' attitudes or, more than likely, they will drift away from you, choosing to continue their negative ways. If this occurs, do not feel bad. Investing in yourself with positivity will pay dividends for a happier life.

After getting a handle on positive thinking, develop the habit of a positive attitude. Be careful to maintain consciousness of your shortcomings. Be humble so as to not come off as egotistical. It is simple for others to confuse positive attitude with conceit or vanity. Attitude is also sometimes misconstrued as superiority or self-centeredness. Radiating a message of *look at me, I am better* is a selfish and self-serving way of being often misinterpreted as a positive attitude. A healthy, modest, unpretentious positive attitude has an air of confidence void of ego and self-centeredness. An optimistic diet of positivity nurtures self-esteem and well-being. Believe in yourself that with patience, you can and will achieve the positivity you need to never give up when facing life's struggles.

The third and final step in becoming a more positive person is to use your positivity to protect and maintain your well-being. Using your positives goes beyond positive thinking and attitude to a higher awareness of what reinforces your positive energy. Identifying your positives involves an introspective search of what makes you tick and feel good. Some examples to help you get started could be family, friends, memories, music, sports, meditation, prayer, and reading. Once you have identified your positives, use them to reinforce your positivity as well as fend off influences of negativity.

To summarize, a healthy positive attitude is the energy of goodness within. Positivity feeds well-being and unselfishly shares good feelings to impact the goodness of others. Follow these three simple steps to positive attitude and energy-filled days.

1. Think positive.
2. Have a positive attitude.
3. Use your positives.

LIFE'S NOTE 46

Faces of Happiness

Happiness is a continuous journey to seek and nurture your heart and mind with happiness. Happiness comes with many faces, from materialism to the influence of positive emotions of our family and those around us. Seeking to achieve happiness with materialism is the path less apt to sustain happiness. Material objects are nice, but they are void of emotional interaction. Instead of chasing objects, embrace family, friends, and others who influence your life in a positive manner, offering love, support, and happiness that endures.

> **Inspiration**
>
> Happiness is appreciating who you are and all the good around us.

Happiness is relative to our upbringing and environment. Memories of happiness range from costly vacations and events to simpler experiences like laughing around a fire pit, playing games, attending family gatherings, pursuing hobbies, going on picnics, and participating in physical outdoor activities. Searching for happiness is easier and more effective if you follow the principle that simpler is better. Keeping your journey simple is far better than complicating things with greed, analysis, or questioning. Be aware of all the good around and within you, and embrace aspects that influence you in a positive way, initiating internal or external smiles.

Happiness does not just appear and happen; we choose to find it. Happiness comes from within. We must create situations along with an open and accepting attitude to initiate a climate rich with opportunities for happiness. Inactivity due to procrastination delays our search for happiness. Stop delaying; take action today to begin your pursuit of happiness. Seeking happiness is a choice and a belief to nurture, achieve, and sustain happiness. Times of joy can last for a few minutes or for days or weeks. This is not to suggest that happiness permeates every moment of every day. Recognize that happiness is more than boisterous laughter, smiles, and fun silliness. Feelings of contentment and comfort support peaceful happiness. Believe and do not give up. Happiness is yours for the taking.

Patience helps us to be realistic as we achieve incremental steps to happiness. Bumps and distractions will periodically surface to hinder our joy. Negativity and skepticism are obstacles, dampening our spirit and making us question our stamina. Draw upon your positives for enthusiasm, motivation, and determination to continue your pursuit and never give up. During your journey, enthusiastic positive attitudes smother the negativity that in the past had a hold on your days. Brighter days of fun, smiles, laughter, comfort, and contentment are just around the corner. Happiness awaits your arrival.

Principles of Happiness

- Take action and begin today.
- Keep it simple.
- Use your positives and stay positive.
- Be enthusiastic.
- Learn from past mistakes.
- Surround yourself with positive people.
- Believe in yourself; do not question yourself.
- Keep expectations simple, realistic, and attainable.
- Feel gratitude for all the goodness within and surrounding you.

Ideas to Achieve Happiness

- Pursue a goal with passion.
- Take up a hobby.
- Find some new interests.
- Make new friends.
- Join a group.
- Keep doing what works and change what is not working.
- Bring back the kid in you.
- Know that silliness is okay—relax.
- Laugh—don't take yourself so seriously.
- Find a career you enjoy—if not, why continue?
- Connect with your spirituality.

LIFE'S NOTE 47

Productivity of Relaxation

When I was growing up, my mom and dad worked hard to provide for my sister and myself. My dad would awake at five o'clock every morning and walk five blocks to the catch the bus in the harsh weather of northern Wisconsin. By 6:00 a.m., he was at a small diner for breakfast to shoot the breeze with his buddies. Work began at seven in the morning and finished at three-fifteen in the afternoon. Mom was also an early riser and home from work at about the same time. Before work and school, Mom and I would listen to the radio and enjoy our breakfast of cereal and toast with peanut butter.

> **Reflection**
>
> Relaxation is being engulfed in an oversize comfy beanbag chair. Stress is trying to get out.

In the late afternoons, we either gathered around the kitchen table or in the living room to talk or watch the news reporting the events of the Vietnam War. Weather permitting, we sat at the picnic table for hours, talking and laughing. On summer nights, my sister and I would sit on a small hill in the backyard, which we called a "bank," with binoculars to watch "silent" movies on the big screen of the Starlite outdoor theater a mile away.

The four of us had fun all year round—fishing from a boat off the shore or ice-fishing, gathering nuts in the woods, playing games, having picnics, camping, or pursuing hobbies, all of which taught us the benefits of relaxation. We found the things we were doing together to be relaxing and learned we need not be alone to relax.

These days, the perception is that there is no longer time to relax. Our careers demand so much more, with fewer people doing more work. No wonder we feel caught up in the concept that every minute we must be productive, both professionally and at home. Most commonly we say we do not have time to relax.

First we should understand that relaxation *is* productive. Why is it that we define relaxing as a waste of time? Taking time for ourselves should be seen as a morsel of dessert each day. Feel the transformation and savor the sweetness of each bite. No matter the day of the week, relax at least three times throughout the day: morning, afternoon, and evening. Waiting until the evening or at bedtime to try to relax for the first time is a bad plan. We think that by crawling into our comfortable cozy bed we can instantly erase the stress and anxiety of the day and relax. But there is too much stored stress and anxiety to deal with just before going to sleep. The usual result is trouble falling asleep and a night of tossing and turning. It's best to have times throughout the day to release pressure. The amount of time to relax is up to us. Start with an allotted amount of time and gradually remove the time limit to wean yourself away from your demanding work schedule. Use this time free of responsibility to reset and recharge.

Learning to relax teaches your body to release tension and stress. Your breathing and heart will slow. You will feel calm. If you have succumbed to the idea that the use of a stress ball will release stress, throw away the stress ball and learn a better way. The stress ball encourages aggression, creating more stress along with tightness as you grip the ball with superhuman strength, attempting to squeeze the daylights out of it. Instead, try closing your eyes and thinking of the positives in your life for a relaxing slice of calm and peace.

How do you begin to relax and not feel guilty for taking time to do it? Begin by making a list of things you do that are free of stress. If you have none, take a power nap or do some silly thing that makes you laugh and smile. Another method is to find someone who knows how to relax and ask for suggestions. Yet another is to reflect on the positives in your life, such as spouse, children, grandchildren, and enthusiasms. Relaxing is productive, as you are doing something to restore and preserve your emotional balance and wellness. Health is best served by preventive health care. Include in your personal health care daily doses of relaxation. You will feel the goodness from relaxing a bit each day. Any guilt from taking time to relax will quickly dissipate, with slices of relaxation incorporated into each day.

Rather than being the patient, be the doctor and write yourself a prescription for relaxation three times a day. Take responsibility to appreciate the benefits of relaxation to minimize the stress and anxiety controlling you and your day.

Benefits of Relaxation

- It releases tension in the body. A relaxed forehead relaxes the mind.
- You slow down emotionally, physically, and biologically.
- Your speech becomes less hurried.
- Your eyes get a rest.
- There's a release of overall tightness.
- Slow motion allows for free thought.
- An optimistic, positive outlook returns.
- A smile replaces a frown, and facial muscles relax.
- You feel happier.

Now is a good time to learn the art of relaxing.

Perspective

Which is more productive; busy-body work, worry, stress—or relaxation?

YOUR NOTES

What stresses you out?

What is your view or opinion of yourself?

Do you know how to relax and take the time to relax?

PART 7

How you perceive life's challenges is usually a crucial obstacle to how you face and overcome them. In this section, insight is shared on how you can better deal with such obstacles. Your mind is most often the worst offender. Learn how to think with your heart to reset your mind so it becomes your greatest asset when facing life's challenges.

LIFE'S NOTE 48

Curveballs of Life

L ike a batter in baseball, we face many pitches throughout our life. Most of the pitches are straightforward, without detours and sudden unexpected changes of direction. However, there is the dreaded curveball with its unexpected change of direction and sinking feeling questioning our ability to handle such a pitch.

Major-league baseball players have difficulty hitting a curveball and other challenging pitches. A batting average of .300 or more is outstanding. Let us consider the .700 of the time those players do not get a hit. An outstanding professional baseball player does not get a hit two and half times more often than he gets one. He might get a walk or a sacrifice fly.

> **Inspiration**
>
> Have the courage to step up to the plate to face life's curveballs to hit them out of the park and run the bases to get back home.

It would be interesting to know the entire population's batting average when facing life's challenges. What percentage of the time are we successful? Also, how long do we idly stand at the plate trying to cope with our challenges? If we mirror the average of a major-league baseball player, we have plenty of room for improvement.

What can we do to improve? The notes in this book tell a story of goodness you can follow to become an all-star. In the same way a baseball player practices at spring training and throughout the season, we too need to practice daily to increase our ability and percentage of success in overcoming life's curveballs.

Follow the message of each note here to find help in facing your challenges. Follow the general theme of goodness to improve your batting average, hit more home runs, and move forward to preserve your well-being.

Some of us are confronted with more of life's curveballs than others. I seem to fall into this category of numerous distractions and challenges. Some of the challenges I have faced are:

- close friend becoming a quadriplegic
- suicide of a close friend
- sudden death of a high-school friend
- parents' cancers
- my own cancer
- my dad's heart failure
- my mom's dementia
- assault of a close friend
- job loss
- trauma of a long-distance relocation
- placing my mother in a nursing home
- my own heart attack

If we compare our lists of distractions or challenges, we may find similar or different situations. Below is a space for listing your past distractions and challenges as well as those you are currently facing. Take ownership of each item. Understand that most often we have no control over the introduction of a distraction. However, it is imperative to take responsibility to care for ourselves to heal and keep stepping up to home plate to get more hits and home runs.

In a previous book, *Finding Your Positives*, I shared a self-help plan for overcoming life's toughest challenges. The theme of *Life's Notes* is to help you live life to its fullest, with goodness permeating your well-being and giving you the ability to handle challenges and preserve balance, harmony, and well-being. Learn from past challenges to face new ones.

Past Challenges   *Current Challenges*

———————————   ———————————

———————————   ———————————

———————————   ———————————

_____   _____

_____   _____

_____   _____

_____   _____

_____   _____

Review your past challenges, appreciate how well you handled them, and gain the confidence to know you can successfully face these situations. Once a current distraction is handled, move it to your list of past distractions to reinforce your confidence and self-esteem. Curveballs will continue to come your way throughout your life. Face the reality that your life may be just fine now, but distractions will happen in the future. Surround and fill yourself with goodness to face future distractions. Step up to the plate to face life's curveballs. Swing the bat to take ownership.

LIFE'S NOTE 49

If It Isn't Something, It's Something Else

L ife continually throws one thing or another our way. It begins shortly after birth—our diaper doesn't get changed as quickly as we would like. Our parents take too long to find our binky. They dress us in funny-looking clothes and we cry, but they have no clue as to why. If it isn't something, it's something else.

Early on in life, we either learn to manage stress, are blessed with the managing-stress gene, or let stress get the best of us and negatively influence our emotions. We begin school and find a new set of somethings. We miss the school bus. We forgot our lunch at home. We are sent to the principal's office and a meeting is scheduled with our parents. We are now six, and all these somethings and more have happened in our short life. You would think that with six years of experience facing these somethings, we would be pros by now to handle these situations stress-free. Not so quick; we're still rookies. We have hundreds and maybe thousands more somethings to face before the curtain closes.

The years pass, and we now have our first car and think we are so hot . . . until we don't have the money for gas or need to pay a $300 speeding ticket or have a fender bender and now car insurance costs $200 a month. The bright side is, we faced some challenging somethings and survived. It could have been worse.

Somethings continue to occur and be annoying, or maybe they get more serious. We have difficulty finding a job. We did not get the promotion. There is a wage freeze at work. Then we are dating, getting engaged, getting married, having children, buying a house. The somethings come more frequently and from numerous directions. The water heater needs to be replaced. There's a plumbing leak. The dog

> **Advice**
>
> *Be not surprised that somethings happen in life. They have before and will again. What matters is how you face these somethings.*

chewed a hole in the sofa. Stress begins to mount. Remember all the numerous somethings we have previously faced to learn from experience and stay in control rather than overanalyze and overreact.

One suggestion is to repeat to yourself the words, "If it isn't something, it's something else" to slow down, calm down, and learn from all our previous somethings that we have survived and will survive this. Be grateful that so far no something has been a serious life challenge.

The house becomes an empty nest and retirement is close at hand. We have a heart attack or are diagnosed with cancer. Now the somethings get more serious. These somethings are not uncommon, as one in two men and one in three women will be diagnosed with cancer sometime during their life. Don't be completely surprised, and try to be prepared as best you can for these serious somethings.

Most somethings are random; others may be genetic or of our own doing. Either way, do not be hard on yourself. Somethings will happen, and we cannot change that fact. Learn to be prepared emotionally to face the somethings that occur in life. Also, understand the common principle that things happen in threes. Experience has shown it to be true. Accept it, deal with it, and move on. Life is too short to stress out over every little something.

LIFE'S NOTE 50

No Big Deal–NBD

Before you initiate or engage in an argument, consider if this conversation is worth your time, effort, and energy. Similar consideration should be used when telling an actual challenge from a nuisance. Too often we react spontaneously before evaluating the possible risk of these situations. There is a way to determine if engaging in an argument

is worthy or if diffusing it before it starts is a better decision. It creates a buffer zone to effectively decide if a situation is truly a challenge to deal with or an annoying nuisance not worthy of attention. The method is called "No Big Deal"—or, abbreviated, "NBD."

The NBD method is simple. Before engaging in an argument or identifying a challenge, ask yourself a few questions: What effect does this situation have on me and others? What are the ramifications of engaging in or dealing with this situation? Does this issue truly matter? Is it worth my time and energy? Actual nuisances cloud our vision and disrupt rational interpretation to confuse them with challenging situations, causing self-induced stress. NBD will reduce the stress and stressful situations in your life.

An argument is usually the result of a conversation gone sour. If the conversation has regressed to an argument, apply the NBD method before continuing engagement. Even if the issue is important to one party, the other party is not obligated to engage. You may be seen as a recreational arguer—someone who enjoys arguing. You may enter into arguments with a winner/loser mentality. Realize that arguing has three possible outcomes: no resolution; compromise; or bitter, bad feelings. With no resolution, there's nothing but heartache. Was the effort worth your time? Was the result frustration and resentment?

A resolution of compromise sounds benign, but do all parties involved see it as benign? Experience and observation would suggest otherwise. Often, one person will falsely agree to compromise to end the argument, preventing hurtful words and heartache. There was perceived compromise, but at least one party feels resentment. Arguing brings out our dark side. As we argue, we raise our voice, interrupt others, and speak hurtful words for the sake of scoring points. Arguing is truly a no-win situation.

When facing potential arguments, follow the NBD method to make wise decisions. The stronger person walks away from an argument while the weaker person is eager to engage with the winner/loser mentality. Explain that you have decided not to engage and that you believe the issue is not worthy of your time or energy. The other person may be upset with you for not engaging. With time, though, he or she may see that arguing is overrated. It is unrealistic to think that relationships will be free of arguments. The hope is they will be less frequent and less intense.

Whereas arguments involve engagement with others, challenges or nuisances are more of a personal matter. Nuisances are things that get under our skin to pester and annoy us. We automatically exaggerate and overreact to these things. Some nuisances might be caused by another's idiosyncrasies and habits, or by situations that are not worth fretting about—family members not closing doors, leaving lights on, or cracking their knuckles, for example. Spills on carpeting, nicks or tears in furniture, and scratches on cars are other examples of nuisances. They may get under our skin, but do they truly matter? Are they worth getting relationships twisted and upset? Rather than being confrontational, calmly use the NBD method to ask what happened and forgive.

If you have identified something as a challenge rather than a nuisance, put a plan in place to deal with it. Challenges are serious matters that seem insurmountable and are best dealt with in a positive way to achieve a healthier outcome. To formulate a positive plan, read or review these notes:

- Embrace the Beauty of Life's Detours
- Life's Busy Intersections
- Labyrinth of Coping
- Three-Day Window to Serenity
- Discovering Positives
- Implementing Positives
- If It Isn't Something, It's Something Else

- Curveballs of Life
- Notes on Cancer

A positive approach is a method for preserving, restoring, and maintaining your well-being for physical, psychological, and emotional balance. Emotional imbalance while facing life's challenges diminishes your chances of overcoming them. Instead, you continue to follow a course of negativity and struggle, with no success in sight. Others can suggest strategies and offer inspiration. However, it is up to you to listen and, most importantly, take action. We are all dealt curveballs in life. Now is the time to hit a home run.

Common Nuisances	*Common Challenges*
idiosyncrasies	disease
leaving lights on	trauma
spills on carpet	loss of loved one
nicks on furniture	divorce
others' driving skills	harassment
slow checkout line	being unappreciated
computer too slow	job loss
price of gas	being overlooked
people who don't say thank you	abuse
the weather	dependency
complainers	emotional issues
	financial loss
	loneliness

LIFE'S NOTE 51

Life's Busy Intersections

L ife is like maneuvering our way along roads and alleys when driving to our destination. Throughout life, we experience stops and starts, sharp turns, and busy intersections. Be thankful for your personal GPS navigation system, your heart.

Most accidents happen at intersections. Difficult impactful decisions at life's intersections define our future and state of well-being. Extreme caution is a must to avoid reacting impulsively. Evaluate your options and choose your direction prudently. Before making

> **Tip**
>
> When coming to a fork in the road, choose the road with the best menu.

your decision, consider and evaluate the impact and consequences of all options, including a U-turn for further evaluation. This process is far removed from choosing which shirt or blouse looks best. Your decision will greatly impact your life, for better or worse. Follow the directions of your heart to steer your life along the road of goodness. Be patient. No one is honking behind you. You control the light.

Yellow is the most important color at a stoplight, and that holds true in life as well for making decisions free of emotional conflict. Caution means to slow down to choose your direction wisely. Which direction you choose could be life-changing. Your heart is your best guide for good decisions. Listen to its voice instead of conflicting emotions to steer along a road of goodness. Don't make a turn for the worse.

Life is not so much about the destination but the inspiring scenic journey along the way. The roads we choose define our internal scenery. When driving down a dark, dreary, bumpy road, stop to take a look at your personal map to reevaluate your course. Why continue along a road with an uninspiring landscape? Opportunities abound at life's intersections to drive roads less traveled, filled with awe-inspiring beauty and breathtaking panoramas. Take time to park at scenic outlooks to appreciate the view, sounds, and smells of nature's beauty. Stay the course of inspiring and nurturing your well-being.

Wellness of heart and soul depends on your ability to make sound, healthy decisions. Reason your decisions out for stability of harmony and balance.

Life's Intersections

- compassion or judgment
- happiness or anger
- moving forward or wallowing in self-pity
- respect or ridicule
- confidence or self-doubt
- positive or negative
- marriage or divorce
- temptation or self-control
- strength to resist or peer pressure
- encouragement or criticism
- motivation or laziness
- passion or boredom
- persevering or giving in
- overcoming or hiding behind obstacles
- hope or despair
- beginning or ending
- faith or disbelief
- courage or weakness

See how making personal choices at life's intersections impacts your life, positive or negative, good or bad. Think of how life might be different if you had chosen a different direction. Listen to your heart. Life's intersections offer options. Choose wisely.

LIFE'S NOTE 52

Dangers of Temptation

The door of temptation is one of the most alluring doors you'll ever confront. It seductively suggests excitement and danger, and we are attracted to its allure and mystery. Opening this door to peek inside, we feel the power of temptation enticing us to cross its threshold. Once inside, we are captivated.

Our desire to participate is so strong we cease to be rational. We twist the truth and imagine this seductive activity is acceptable so as to approve our behavior. We become blind to the danger signs, lose sight of our moral values, and think only of ourselves. Succumbing to temptation is selfish behavior. It's all about *me*, ignoring consideration for others.

> **Tip**
>
> Heed the danger signs of temptations to follow the road of straight and narrow.

Giving in to temptation without question is behavior of *I* and *me*. Our morals and sense of *we* and *us* are lost in our uncontrollable desire to abandon self-control. Our mind is short-circuited to override our ability to distinguish between right and wrong or good and bad. The focus of our decision is solely self-centered, with little or no consideration for those we love.

The question of how and why we give in to temptation seems perplexing, but it's really quite simple. Selfishness, peer pressure, and curiosity build up over time to a wave that pushes us over the top to act upon our desires. Our weaknesses of discipline and character are exposed. We are excited, and it feeds our ego until we're blinded to any repercussions.

There are things you can do to walk away from the door of temptation.

- Avoid placing yourself in the presence of seductive temptation. Stay away from environments or activities likely to manipulate thought, desire, and wild imagination.
- The moment you feel the allure of temptation to alter your thoughts, call immediately on the moral compass of your heart.

If a temptation has any negative connotations, which they all do, you need to understand the harm and risk to relationships, to loved ones, friends, and yourself, both emotionally and physically.

- Use your moral barometer to think of *we* and *us*, rather than *I* and *me*. You have a responsibility to act with consideration, kindness, and love for others to preserve and grow your relationships.
- Rely on your spirituality to direct you away from wrongful, bad, and evil behavior. Spirituality realigns our thoughts to accountability and responsibility, not only to ourselves but for those we love and care for. Life is about how we give of ourselves, not how we take away from others. The risk of temptation is so great and the repercussions so severe that any benefits are shallow, hollow, and oh so selfish.

When facing temptation, ask yourself this one question: Am I willing to engage in life-altering behavior with drastic repercussions? If you have reservations of any kind, it is time to walk away.

The stronger person walks away while the weak succumb to peer pressure, desire, and curiosity. The strong have no regrets as they walk away, while the weak are regretful for their actions and disappointed in themselves. To understand the selfish allure of temptation, it is helpful to consider a few examples.

Smoking is a door of temptation we often face as adolescents. We are with a group of so-called friends, and some of them are smoking. They ask us to try a cigarette. There is a share of us that during our adolescent years probably perceived smoking as being cool. We quickly rationalize that we can try one cigarette and if we don't like it, no more. However, peer pressure and the addictive chemicals pull us in so tight we are unable to escape its grasp. Smoking is certainly life-altering behavior for ourselves and for those within the cloud of secondhand smoke, as well as the obnoxious smell we ask others to tolerate around the house and in the car.

Drugs and smoking share the commonality of addiction as well as emotional and physical harm to us and others. Drugs prey on the emotionally weak, from those who are down and out to the financially secure who are in emotional chaos. It takes a strong person to walk away.

Those who do break free from drugs and smoking avoid the dangerous life-altering behavior that shortens their life and robs it of quality.

Alcohol in excess is a temptation with repercussions to self and loved ones. It goes against our self-defined parameters of moderation and excess. Most often the vision of the one using alcohol is blurred to weigh on the side of moderation. This is classic denial. The more reliable evaluation of moderation or excess is defined by loved ones and friends. Sometimes they care more about the alcohol-abuser than the alcohol-abuser cares for himself or herself.

Drugs and alcohol have been responsible for disrupting and destroying families and relationships. Those who choose drugs or alcohol are prone to abusive behavior—emotional, verbal, psychological, physical, or financial. Please, at all costs, avoid the door of drugs and alcohol. Both are life-altering choices with drastic ramifications. Doing drugs and consuming excessive amounts of alcohol can lead to downward spirals. Many of us are unable to escape, resulting in aging faster or, worse yet, dying prematurely.

Adultery or sexual promiscuity are selfish behaviors that also have dramatic life-altering ramifications. Sexual promiscuity lowers our opinion of ourselves. It also invites emotional chaos and disease. Adultery is selfish behavior, putting aside our accountability and responsibility for our spouse and loved ones and instead thinking only of ourselves. When facing the door of adultery, do not even think of reaching for the handle to peek inside. Instead, turn your back to the door and think with your heart about the life-altering repercussions. Your spouse and your family love you and depend on you. Walk away to show love for them and yourself.

Overindulgence of any kind negatively influences behavior and relationships. Eating to excess or uncontrollable eating patterns develop control over our opinion of ourselves, and have detrimental results to our health. Overindulgence of desire for monetary and materialistic wealth fosters uncontrollable want, leading to greed at all costs to reach a self-defined pinnacle of achievement. Magnified indulgence of any kind that takes away time from family and relationships is indulgence of self, demonstrating blindness to our loved ones' needs. Overindulgence is another life-altering choice that can be avoided by not opening that door.

Professional and amateur athletes have shown a pattern of succumbing to the temptation of performance-enhancing drugs. They rationalize their behavior by thinking *others do it so I have to so I can compete*. This thought process reminds us of how others are wearing a certain brand of clothes, so we think we must do so to be cool. This analogy illustrates how easy it is to rationalize indulging in tempting behavior before recognizing our weaknesses and taking precautionary steps to consider our opinion of ourselves. In fairness to athletes, some organizations have made strides and reduced the use of performance-enhancing drugs. However, there is more work to be done.

When facing a door of temptation, draw upon your morals and spirituality to choose between right and wrong, good and bad, moral and evil. The process by which we decide is the conflict. Do we choose to think with mind or heart? Do we consider the repercussions of engaging? Do we consider our responsibility and accountability to loved ones and friends? The best barometer is to remember that life is not all about us. It is about how we responsibly give of ourselves to those we love and cherish.

LIFE'S NOTE 53

Embrace the Beauty of Life's Detours

Life follows the directions on our map of where we want or hope to go. We can arrive at our destination in an efficient methodical way or continue to drift along aimlessly. No matter how we get there, we become comfortable with our mode of transportation, our schedule, and the usual scenery. We prefer the familiarity and predictability of our route. Bumps, hills, and detours remove us from our comfort zone, creating confusion and doubt as to how to deal with this unfamiliar road.

> **Inspiration**
>
> Life's detours, though possibly tough, seen from an optimistic perspective offer opportunity to further discover yourself to go beyond and achieve greater heights.

Detours are life's way of redirecting us to new scenery, new people, and new opportunities. Don't become discouraged, as life will unexpectedly direct us to many detours. Our perception of a detour forecasts how well we navigate the twists and turns and how well we emerge at the end. How we approach a detour—as an obstacle, pain, problem, nuisance, opportunity, or adventure—influences how we suffer through or benefit from this new path.

At the beginning of each detour, there is a sign or a flag for us to stop or slow down. This pause before entering a detour gives us time to think in slow motion to evaluate, absorb, and accept this path of redirection. Also to our advantage is a slower speed limit, encouraging us to take our time and settle in to slowly become comfortable along the way. There is no set timetable maneuvering a detour. Stop at a lookout periodically to pause and accept this path and what it has to offer.

Life's detours are not always brief and smooth. Some are far longer and rougher to navigate. The scenery may not be to our liking, and the fog blurs our vision to keep us from seeing any opportunities. However, detours offer new scenery for us to find beauty and appreciate it; to open our eyes, mind, and heart; to express gratitude; and to move forward along our journey. Embrace the newfound beauty of a detour to emerge a better and stronger person.

Detours are life's way of redirecting us to heightened awareness, compassion, gratitude, inspiration, and forgiveness. Detours are not paths leading nowhere. Instead, they are a course of enlightenment and strength, leading us to discover and persevere for a better us.

No matter how smooth and short the path or how long and bumpy the detour, embrace the journey rather than fight it. Stay the course and do not give up. We will get back on track.

Some Detours

- finances
- job loss
- divorce
- death of loved one
- health issues
- trauma—physical, emotional, or verbal
- coping due to a difficult event
- loneliness
- stress
- anxiety
- depression
- aging
- caregiving

Have an awareness of the scenery on life's detours. It could present opportunities.

LIFE'S NOTE 54

Artistry of Aging

There are doors we enthusiastically open and doors we choose not to. Aging is most likely one of the doors we choose to avoid. Yet it seems to have an inevitable automatic door opener pulling us in. Some cross this threshold sooner in life than others because of genetic, physical, environmental, or state-of-mind influences.

> **Inspiration**
>
> Artistry of aging is the experience to appreciate the beauty of each day to play and live with gratitude.

When facing the door of aging, we have a choice to open it or let it remain closed, hoping to delay aging. Our mindset has much to do with this choice. There is no right or wrong decision. However, when facing this door, approach it cautiously. Consider spending extended time on the porch before crossing the threshold to slow its grasp and its possible accelerating effects. Once we cross aging's threshold, we must accept the progression of aging as our new normal.

Accepting that aging is a natural phenomenon of life does not necessarily correlate to allowing it to affect your attitude or alter your state of mind to contentment with aging. You can continue to have a young, spirited approach and think younger if it makes you more enthusiastic and energetic. We often hear that getting old is a state of mind. Do what you can to slow down or, in some cases, delay the progression of aging by adopting an optimistic, positive attitude.

Often, aging does not come in a nicely wrapped package with a beautiful bow. Aging's multiple facets throw curveballs our way, attempting to accelerate the aging process. These can be physical, emotional, or genetic. Understanding these obstacles is helpful in managing your mind and spirit to age with an enthusiastic gusto for life.

Physical challenges restrict mobility or sensory capacity. At times, these challenges can feel overwhelming to the point of controlling our mind and days. Yes, we do have a new normal. Do not give in to these challenges. Discover the strength and will to adapt. You need not accept these limitations as inevitabilities of aging. Explore life from different perspectives to discover new avenues to ignite your spirit for fresh new passions. Embrace life, as there is so much yet to explore and discover. Your means of exploration could be different from those of the past, yet possibly more complete and just as exciting. What remains important is that you continue to explore and discover to reach the pinnacle of your work and enjoy your accomplishments. Celebrate each moment of discovery and achievement.

Emotions contribute more to our psyche than we would like to accept. Psyche is often referred to as our state of well-being, which in turn influences how we choose to live each day and deal with life's obstacles. Our emotions paint a picture, and it is up to the mind to interpret the meaning of the painting, thus establishing our psyche or emotional status. For example, if we are feeling sad, our canvas will most likely reflect those negative feelings. If we are stressed, our picture will be chaotic. If we feel depressed, our painting will depict loneliness and possibly hopelessness. We begin to see how our emotions have a direct effect on our well-being and how our emotions influence how we choose to face aging.

Struggling with the personal experiences of cancer and a heart attack opened my eyes and heart to the masterpiece I was painting each and every day. You are the artist controlling the brush and hues of your day. Try more positive brush strokes and vibrant colors to spread optimism, curb the progression of aging, and celebrate its beauty of enlightenment.

Every week, scientists discover more about the role that genes play in our biology and the ticking of our biological clock. Some conditions offer little if any control to slow our clock, such as Alzheimer's, dementia, and some cancers. There are diseases that dim or shade areas of the mind, slowing our memory and thought processes as well as darkening our will. Genetics does play a significant biological role in our aging process that cannot be denied. Our mother's experience with dementia taught our family that the mind may have been weakened but the heart can remain strong. Cherish and incorporate the strength of your spirit and heart to enjoy and appreciate each day.

Aging's combination of physical, emotional, and genetic facets, if timidly accepted, can negatively influence your mind and heart to adopt a state of pessimism and negativity to succumb at the door of aging. With healthy well-being and a positive state of mind and heart, you can delay the emotional state of aging and walk through the door with confidence to slow its effects and live life with quality and enthusiastic energy.

LIFE'S NOTE 55

Steps to Move Forward from Traumatic Events

The next seven notes share insight from my personal experience with cancer. The theme of these combined notes offers advice you can use to ease the pain and struggle associated with the challenge of coping with life's traumatic events.

These notes offer steps to navigate through the many emotions people face during sudden, life-altering events. These steps were developed from years of experience and will help others adopt a fresh perspective to maintain control and to continue living life with enthusiasm and passion. Life may have changed but rest assured, with strength, patience, and persistence you will reach a higher spiritual level of consciousness, awareness, and appreciation.

> **Tip**
>
> *Facing the aftermath of life's traumatic events is all about your decisions to move forward or stand still.*

The steps can be applied to any challenging obstacle you face. It is recommended to pair these steps with assistance from a professional therapist or counselor to overcome and recover from a traumatic event.

Provide your obstacles in the inserts below with which you struggle to cope.

Seven Steps:

_____—What Now?   _____—Ending or Beginning

_____—Coming to Terms   _____—Small Wins

_____—Ownership   _____—Live

_____—Acceptance

LIFE'S NOTE 56

Cancer—What Now?

From the moment you hear you have cancer, you think: *What now? What should I do? Where do I begin? Why me?* and *How do I deal with this?* All good questions, but at the same time, they cause confusion and provide no answers. Yet your mind says you need answers. Your heart looks for comfort. Your soul searches for peace.

> **Tip**
>
> Let the shock subside to realize you can be controlled by fear or you can use hope and faith to control your fear.

There are no right or wrong answers about how to react to or cope with cancer. However, some answers are more beneficial to our emotional well-being than others. Differentiating among the possible answers to determine which will serve us best can be a difficult task.

Cancer scares us with the uncertainty of the unknown. We feel uncomfortable and fearful. Our well-being had been protected with structure and order, guiding life with calmness and comfort. Now there is only disorder, disarray, and imbalance. If left to run rampant, the chaos will take over, with conflicting thoughts infesting our well-being.

Fear, if left unchecked, leads to anger, intense stress, and possibly depression, all leading down a dark path. Fear clouds our vision and ability to function in a disciplined way to protect our emotional well-being. Learning to manage and control fear changes our journey and our quality of life.

It is easy to become obsessed with *amount* of time rather than *quality* of time. Cancer presents each of us with the opportunity to perceive our life as a gift to appreciate each day. Instead of continuing to look far into the future, cherish each day as a gift and live it to its fullest. Express gratitude for each and every day. Seize this opportunity to live with quality of life rather than focusing on quantity of time.

Living each day as a gift changes our outlook from despair to peace and hope. Many of us allow Mother Nature's weather to influence our attitude. Instead, ignore the external weather and read your internal weather. The weather outside should have no influence. Each and every day, forecast your personal weather as a beautiful day to be enjoyed. Too often we are discouraged if a planned activity was dampened by Mother Nature. Learn to adapt, as you have no control over the weather outside. All you can control is your personal weather.

Adaptation is fundamental to learning to deal with the struggle of coping day after day. Focus on positivity and gratitude to ease the fear and discomfort of cancer, which are only intensified by continued negativity. Sharing your thoughts and feelings with others opens your heart and mind to alternative courses, directing you to ways to adapt and cope. Our ability to adapt contributes to protecting us from emotional paralysis.

Cancer need not be constantly scary. Discover an enlightened consciousness to identify and appreciate all you have and the goodness around you. Your heart and mind are free now to think deeper than before, to understand what truly matters in life and what is trivial. Family relationships and friendships grow stronger. The bonds become deeper and more appreciated. We only get better. Acceptance of cancer is a step to taking ownership of it and dealing with the challenges of the journey.

Life's Note 57

Cancer–Coming to Terms

Cancer can throw you for a loop, especially when you first hear the words, "Sorry, you have cancer." News like this initially shocks the system. You feel numb or petrified, followed by further confusing and conflicting emotions. An emotional roller-coaster ride like this needs immediate attention to smooth the bumps and valleys, clear the dizziness, slow down, and assess your new challenge.

This cancer-related series of notes was developed from my personal experience with cancer—from hearing my test was positive to being a cancer survivor today. These notes are steps to help you navigate your way through the labyrinth of emotions along your journey of trials, tribulations, and triumphs for brighter days of calm, comfort, and peace.

> **Advice**
>
> Instead of asking why me, ask why not me. This will help to understand that cancer offers the opportunity to improve our perspective for positive effects to cope better.

One in two men and one in three women will be diagnosed with cancer at some time during their life. Nearly everybody will be touched or influenced by coming to terms with the diagnosis of cancer in a family member, friend, neighbor, or coworker.

Learn how to take ownership and choose paths wisely. Learn acceptance to move forward, to benefit from victories, and to continue to enjoy life. Yes, you have been thrown a curveball. Understand how to take control to preserve and awaken who you are and appreciate all the goodness within and surrounding you to make the most of each and every day. Learn the "Three-Day Window to Serenity" method (Note 67) and live today to illuminate the dawn of tomorrow.

Becoming a caregiver for a loved one or friend with cancer is also addressed. Ideas are shared to help you begin to understand your importance and the benefits of support for you and the loved one needing care. Learn how to be a caregiver to provide support and be comfortable without fear of doing wrong. Discover how this new responsibility offers the opportunity for a deeper bond between you and the one you care for while working through this new challenge.

If you or a loved one is diagnosed with cancer or you become a caregiver, I wish you and your caregiving support network all the best along your journey from acceptance and coping to brighter days of happiness. Coming to terms with cancer is ownership to cope, recover, and live free of its grasp.

LIFE'S NOTE 58

Cancer—Ownership

Now that you are facing the challenge of cancer, consider formulating a plan. You will be taking a solid step to beat cancer by taking ownership. That's right: take ownership, and the earlier the better. Establish ownership after testing or shortly after diagnosis and prior to treatment.

Your journey is personal. Be active in all decisions with research, spirituality, the stories of others, support groups, and professionals. Being involved helps you to manage your consternation, numbness, fears, and uncertainty. Time slows down to see things clearer and to think in slow-motion. For many, this heightened awareness enhances your thought process to think with your heart as well as your mind. What follows is a deeper appreciation for all you have and gratitude for those who love and care for you. Compassion replaces judgment for understanding the challenges others are facing and empathy for their struggle. When following compassion you will find comfort and strength from not judging yourself and empathy for yourself. Discover that cancer need not be an ending. Embrace the challenge and choose your path as a beginning to something new.

With ownership, you gain realistic expectations. That's not to say you don't want to live to be one hundred. A small percentage of us will reach this milestone. Just be realistic. An extended life, no matter how long, is a gift to be cherished. Express gratitude for this gift, as it is not about length of time but how we live our time. This concept of quality of time compared to quantity of time is difficult to grasp. Once you accept this concept, you'll find a sense of peace and comfort to relish the beauty of today. Furthermore, you'll replace the edginess of anxiety and worry with calming peace and control to live the future to its fullest. Give cancer a bear hug as you take ownership, and let it know it is no longer the boss.

> **Tip**
>
> When all seems darkest, we most need a leader. There is no one better than you.

Ownership involves taking action, responsibility, discipline, accountability, and inspiration to beat cancer and cope with all that entails. One of the challenges of coping is allowing cancer to consume and control our days. Another issue is people continually asking us questions related to our cancer. Be gentle, but do inform them that you are interested in topics other than cancer. They will appreciate your honesty in helping them feel comfortable to approach you without fear of saying something inappropriate or offensive. If someone does say something that bothers you, does it truly warrant a response, or is forgiveness a better path? Making wise decisions from your heart is a step toward taking ownership of cancer, lifting your spirits, and forecasting positive daily personal weather. Learn to live today to illuminate tomorrow. Remember the elements of ownership.

- *Action*: Without action, moving forward is difficult at best. Negativity sets in.
- *Responsibility*: Measure your well-being and see if you need to do more.
- *Discipline*: Find motivation to continue your ownership each and every day, and never give in to cancer.
- *Accountability*: With ownership, you become accountable to yourself. Don't give up.
- *Inspiration*: Inspire yourself each day to inspire others for appreciation and gratitude.

Show compassion to your loved ones and caregivers, as they too are experiencing a wide array of emotions. With family and support come strength, and with strength comes wins, and with wins come peace and serenity. Taking ownership helps to formulate a plan and gives peace and comfort to your journey.

LIFE'S NOTE 59

Cancer—Acceptance

Cancer is no fun, but you must face it as best you can. Continuing to wallow in the muck and mire of pity is a dreary road of dismal days filled with negativity and sadness. In an effort to begin to manage your emotions to accept that you have cancer, you must do what is necessary to move forward. This is easier said than done.

Advice

Accept the fact that you have cancer, as it can't be changed. Accept that you have control. Accept that with hope and faith you will have wins.

Acceptance can come shortly after diagnosis or after a period of adjustment. There is no prescribed timetable for attempting to adjust. You must gather your wits and somehow try to relax and make a plan to face your cancer. With this approach, you start to establish a foundation for a better way to cope on your road through treatment and recovery.

Acceptance calms your emotions to a manageable state for a sense of relief and comfort. You have acknowledged the fact that you have cancer and cannot change that fact. There is peace in being free of emotions like denial and pity. Freedom feels far better than the continued confinement of stress, anger, anxiety, and worry. This is not to say these emotions will never resurface, but when they do, their impact will be less severe.

To worry about a recurrence of cancer hinders your ability to cope and live each day. The probability of cancer reoccurring is primarily out of your control. Fear of cancer coming back contributes to worry and stress, putting your well-being out of balance. If you have no control over the situation, do not waste time and energy trying to change it. Instead, invest your time and energy in achieving positivity for personal growth and gratitude. Take command of your journey to conquer cancer and live life abundantly.

Acceptance is freedom to take command of your journey. With acceptance, you can achieve more than you ever thought. You set the rules for the new normal. Days will be brighter and the journey will enlighten you to find and use your positives for well-being and purpose. Acceptance makes your path smoother for footprints of peace and hope.

LIFE'S NOTE 60

Cancer—Ending or Beginning

When faced with cancer, one of life's toughest challenges, most of us are unsure how to react. While waiting four weeks before hearing the results of my biopsy, I thought I had prepared myself for either good news or not-so-good news. I first felt numb when I heard the words, "You have cancer." I wasn't sad or angry or self-pitying. Feeling numb was a weird feeling, as I didn't know what to do or how to react. This may have been more of a struggle than releasing some emotions.

> **Inspiration**
>
> *Cancer stinks, but you control the fragrance of your journey.*

I let a few days pass to allow my new challenge to settle in and focus my thoughts for a plan of action. I had a rough idea to use my personal positives to face this challenge. I knew I could control my journey and make decisions to follow the path to a new beginning. When facing a challenge, we either consciously or subconsciously follow a course of action, choosing an ending or a new beginning to cope day to day. One of the wisest decisions I made was choosing to see my journey to beat cancer as a new beginning. This decision immediately infused me with hope, courage, motivation, and positivity to approach each day as a win. Coping was far less stressful, as I had a plan for managing my emotions.

There is no right or wrong choice to make. At any given moment, you make a decision that seems right at the time. I preferred the path of a new beginning, as it focused on positives like hope, patience, inspiration, and an open heart. The path of an ending, on the other hand, focuses on hopelessness, loneliness, stress, worry, pity, anxiety, and a cold negative heart. This path can make your challenge seem insurmountable, to the point of giving up before you even start to take the steps to cope with and beat your challenge.

The paths of ending or new beginning are not parallel paths. They intertwine, inviting us to a new beginning or tempting us to select the path of "Why me?" If you initially choose the course of an ending and then venture to a new beginning, you will find, as I did, the path of a new beginning to be a more peaceful and hopeful journey. On the other hand, if you start out for a beginning and stumble onto the path of an ending with all its negativity, you will want to return to the welcome and warmth of a new beginning. I didn't even consider the path of an ending. Giving up was never an option.

The path of a new beginning is not an easy road. There are bumps along the way. With patience, perseverance, and persistence, you will emerge from the shadows of despair and hopelessness to victory and brighter days ahead. This path also opens the heart and revitalizes passion to reach out and help others with their struggles.

Now, whenever I face a new challenge, I always point my journey along the path of a new beginning. Next time you are challenged, try starting with a new beginning to cope and eventually overcome. I believe you will find yourself becoming a better and stronger person, more aware of all that is good around you and with a greater appreciation for all we have.

The choice is yours, an ending or a new beginning. Choose wisely, as your choice defines your journey.

LIFE'S NOTE 61

Cancer—Small Wins

The approach many take is to beat cancer, and rightfully so. Some hope and pray for a miracle, and we hope they are blessed with one. Another plan to deal with cancer is to focus on small and frequent wins throughout our journey.

These modest victories motivate and inspire us to seek more and more opportunities to win. The more the wins add up, the more positive our spirits and our days. We are less apt to give in and let cancer control us. Instead, we control our attitude and journey. Numerous small wins foster confidence to accept and take ownership of our cancer and live our lives.

What does it mean to have a "win" with cancer? Ultimately, it is to be a survivor and cancer-free. Certainly this is the biggest win. However, realistically, this may be a reach for some diagnosed with cancer. Extending life by any amount of time can be a win. Just taking ownership of cancer is a win. This is not to diminish the power of hope or suggest giving up. The purpose is to feel comfort knowing you can meet cancer face to face and win.

These smaller wins are no less impactful than the greater victories we celebrate. Once you begin to think with your heart, the so-called smaller wins become more recognizable and appreciated. Your heart feels their influence in setting your emotional direction. To help you recognize and appreciate the smaller wins, some possibilities are listed below.

> **Tip**
>
> The value of a win over life's struggles is to see what truly matters in life.

> **Inspiration**
>
> Spirit kindles desire.
> Desire fans will.
> Will lights determination.
> Determination fires wins.

- Watch how your family and friends rally to support you. You win.

- Gain a deeper connection with your spouse, partner, and loved ones. You win.
- Look at the compassion of your doctors, nurses, technicians, and support people. Connect with them to express compassion and gratitude. You win.

- Look forward to treatments, no matter how difficult, as you are one day closer to extending your life. Each day, you win.
- Side effects, though tough, are proof that treatment is doing its work. You win.
- Observe others with tough challenges, not only cancer, to see their strengths or difficulties. Look in a mirror and reflect on how you choose to cope. You win.
- Feel a heightened awareness and appreciation of all the good that surrounds you. You win.
- Be grateful for all your blessings. They may be difficult to find at a time like this, but take time to look deeper. The blessings are there. You win.
- Find new interests and passions. You win.

Have the awareness to recognize and celebrate wins along your way.

LIFE'S NOTE 62

Cancer—Live

The controlling grasp cancer has on our days makes it difficult to find some fun. Maybe you're thinking, "How can you have fun with cancer?" You're right, it can be difficult. Cancer's smothering effects are no fun at all. However, cancer doesn't mean you can never have fun again. If you're no longer having fun, the decision is yours. Do not give in to cancer's control. Try a new approach to make each day a "Funday."

> **Tip**
>
> To ease the pain and fear from cancer's emotional grasp, live each day a Funday with smiles, laughter, and silliness.

Yes, you can have a week with seven Fundays. Start with one day, and then another and another. Mixing an ounce of fun into your routine is magical. Watch the transformation in your days and yourself.

What is a Funday? A Funday is a day in which you find any sort of place to smile, laugh, and be happy and silly. Fun is the things you do that raise your spirits, put happiness in your heart, add joy to your voice, let music ring in your ears, and keep your funny bone jiggling. Now go have some fun.

Begin by loosening the collar of cancer's control. Stop thinking about cancer every moment of every day. Just as you find some time to eat every day, you can find some time to feed your being with smiles and laughter.

Certainly there will be days that are not as fun as others. The point is to find even a smidgen of fun in every day. Days of treatment could be difficult, with accompanying side effects making it seem impossible to find anything funny. You must challenge yourself to find a pinch of fun. When you do find it, even if only for a brief moment, enjoy the weightless feeling from the stressful gravity of cancer. Celebrate that moment. Congratulations, you did it! You had a Funday.

A Funday is not a day of all play and laughter. Be realistic and recognize that even brief moments of happiness add up to goodness from smiles and laughter. The inspiration of our Funday encourages us to live each day with less heartache for increased comfort both physically and emotionally.

On a Funday, coping becomes less of a struggle. You become more relaxed or learn how to relax. Cancer is no longer the boss of you. You are in control. Now go and live each day as a Funday. Smile big, laugh loud, make noise, sing loud, and dance often. Enjoy breaks for relaxation. You can do it. Find some fun. Live today to illuminate the dawn of tomorrow.

LIFE'S NOTE 63

Labyrinth of Coping

Coping is a puzzle much like a labyrinth, with walls obstructing your view. The good news is that the labyrinth of coping has doors leading to freedom. They may be few and frustrating to find. However, do not be discouraged. The doors are there; you just need the motivation and discipline to navigate to a door and free yourself from the emotional struggle of coping. Do not give up.

> **Advice**
>
> *How you choose to cope makes all the difference.*

A labyrinth has walls and a floor, but no ceiling. The walls might feel confining and suffocating, but when you look up, you can take a breath of fresh air and be warmed by the sun. As with a labyrinth, coping also requires patience, persistence, and perseverance to find the way to freedom.

Along the way, the sky may grow dark, with ominous storm clouds. Pause to relax, as you have the ability to change the weather. Be aware that you are the one creating the storms over the labyrinth of coping. How you live each day determines the forecast for tomorrow. If your days continue to be cloudy and stormy, review how you have lived the day before. Alter your attitude to surround yourself with more positivity. It is positivity that gives you a weather forecast of warm, sunny days. The sunshine lights the labyrinth, making it easier for you to maneuver through the twisting corridors and manage your stress and anxiety.

Dark days can lead to continued paths of frustration, loneliness, and hopelessness. Review each day to escape these dreary negative paths. Be completely honest when assessing your situation so as not to cheat yourself of progress toward a door of freedom. You can see your journey of coping as an ending or a new beginning. Choose wisely.

Coping is a puzzle of many pieces with sharp, jagged edges. Work by connecting only two pieces at any given time. This keeps you from sprinting to find a door and missing connecting pieces along the way. A puzzle is not complete until the last piece is in place. The number of pieces will vary from person to person and challenge to challenge. Any time you connect another piece is a victory to be celebrated. Each connection offers inspiration to be persistent, to continue to move forward, and to not give up.

You will find a door to freedom from the day-to-day struggle of coping. Finding your positives and using them along the way will help you achieve your goal of overcoming your challenge. Walk one step at a time to your door of freedom.

LIFE'S NOTE 64

Caregiving Is the Culmination of Love

When we are young, we rarely give any thought to caregiving because of our sense of youth and invincibility. Our common response to someone hurting is to say, "I know someone who had this, you'll be fine, it just takes time." We have a tendency to pass judgment before considering compassion. Various situations occur in life when becoming a caregiver is suddenly expected or simply the right thing to

> ## Perspective
>
> *Caregiving is from love, not obligation; compassion, not judgment; patience, not intolerance; and commitment, not a pastime.*

do, and then our perspective changes. Parenting, trauma to a loved one, aging, disease, and the death of a loved one are obvious times when the responsibility of becoming a caregiver is thrust upon us.

Parenting is the most basic, yet the most complicated and one of the most rewarding times to nurture and expand our skills as a caregiver. Parenting teaches us to be caregivers out of love, not obligation; compassion, not judgment; patience, not intolerance; and commitment, not a pastime. Relatives share the same responsibility as parents, with the luxury of shorter hours and restful nights.

Trauma and disease to a loved one are unexpected situations when, without warning or preparation, we must become caregivers and learn the skills on the job. There is no time for the luxury of a training period; caring begins *now*. Love, compassion, patience, and commitment are attributes that best serve the one needing care as well as the one providing it. The need for caregiving has many forms, including trauma occurring at birth, accidents, addiction, disease, and abuse. Each form has its own unique challenges. Do your best to be adaptive, flexible, and patient with yourself. Your heart is your best guide.

Aging presents a myriad of challenges requiring care. Your parents cared for you from birth through your teenage years and beyond, and now it is time to return the favor and take the responsibility to care for them in their time of need. Someday we, too, will face the challenges of aging for which assistance would be appreciated. Caring for the elderly presents an opportunity to awaken and deepen relationships to a greater consciousness of meaning and purpose. Appreciate and cherish the time together.

The death of a loved, whether gradual or sudden, brings with it the unique challenge of coping with finality. Sudden death, particularly the death of a child, shocks people so deeply that emotions seem insurmountable. Making sense of it all is difficult at best. Caregiving is as important with the death of a loved one as with any other situation. Only now the caregiving is for a group of people mourning and dealing with their loss. Caregiving becomes a team effort to lean on each other for support to begin the process of healing.

Caregiving has times of trials and tribulations, as well as times of reward and celebration. It is by no means a smooth and happy road; in fact, it can be rough with emotions needing mending. It is natural to feel uncomfortable and uneasy when providing care. Do not feel stressed or inadequate; you will do just fine.

Caregiving, depending on the situation, presents unique needs for specific care—from basic cleanliness to rehabilitation, to hugs, smiles, and kindness. Do not let nervousness or self-doubt make you question your ability to provide care. Believe in yourself and rest assured you will be valuable to the one receiving care. You will do more than you'll ever realize.

Over time, a deeper bond will form through the relationship of caregiving. Together you will share emotional highs and lows as well as setbacks and victories, accompanied by sadness and joy and most of all love. You will discover that you are truly a gift to one another. Sometimes it takes becoming a caregiver to open your heart to share your gift. If this is so, be grateful for this opportunity. The person being cared for will be forever appreciative and grateful that you were there. Both of you will be changed forever. Cherish the shared time and memories. The experience of caregiving will serve you well when called upon in the future to face life's challenges and care for others.

Tips for Caregivers

- Know that what you do has no rights or wrongs. Don't be hard on yourself.
- Have patience and confidence.
- Be sensitive to the person's wants and needs.
- Customize care to the personality and strengths of the person you're caring for.
- Be honest with the feelings of all involved.
- Create some quality time.
- Be respectful.
- Protect dignity.
- Care as an equal.
- Talk with other caregivers.
- Show genuine interest in the person you're caring for. Engage in conversation.
- Meals can be important times of day.
- Have compassion and empathy.
- Have genuine interest in the person's story.
- Nurture your own well-being.
- Manage tasks and time. Do your best and you'll be fine.
- Be organized. Keep notes, especially about medications. A calendar or journal seems to work best.
- Maintain supplies.
- Share the responsibilities with others. There is strength in numbers.
- Find time for yourself. Treat yourself now and then.

Inspiration

Love is lifting people up in time of need.

LIFE'S NOTE 65

Discovering Positives

Each of us has an untapped reserve of gold nuggets lying deep within, waiting to be discovered. All that is necessary to discover these nuggets is exploration and honesty. Wear a miner's helmet with its bright light to explore your heart and soul and mine golden nuggets of positivity. Honesty from the heart is the tool best suited to identifying our positives. Our gold reserve is rich beyond our expectations.

> **Tip**
>
> Discover that which makes you feel good about yourself: your inner positives.

As we discover these golden nuggets of positivity, we clear away the sediment that has clouded our vision. Nuggets are things in our life that deeply touch our heart and soul. Some are tangible; others are intangible. They give purpose to our life and define the core of our well-being. Positives maintain and, if necessary, restore emotional balance and harmony for healthy, meaningful well-being. Shining our miner's lamp to discover our potential positives is an essential step to evaluating the effect these nuggets have on our life and the way each one helps us through tough times.

Chemistry uses a Periodic Table of the Elements (also discussed in Note 3) as the basis for equations and experiments. With that as inspiration, I've devised a Table of Potential Positives to help you excavate your nuggets of gold.

> **Inspiration**
>
> Our positives are those things that inspire self.

Table of Potential Positives

Family	Children	Grandchildren	Spouse
Parents	Sister	Brother	Relatives
Memories	Spirituality	Prayer	Meditation
Inspiration	Mentoring	Friends	Volunteering
Exercise	Yoga	Music	Reading
Musical Instrument	Good Deeds	Writing	Painting
Theater	Singing	Dancing	Acting
Learning	Cooking	Picnics	Family Events
Helping Others	Donating	Giving Back	Walking
Pets	Gardening	Flowers	Landscaping
Woodworking	Working on Cars	Hunting	Fishing
Hiking	Bicycling	Barbeques	Celebrations

LIFE'S NOTE 66

Implementing Positives

The plan to discover and implement your golden nuggets of positivity goes beyond positive thinking. This is a two-step process requiring action, responsibility, accountability, and measurability. Positive thinking alone was not enough to help me manage and overcome my challenges. I needed something more structured than an attitude of, "I can do this." Through trial and error, I realized I needed action as well as thought.

> **Inspiration**
>
> When the burden weighs heavy, your inner positives bring strength to restore smiles and peace to celebrate life.

I began to learn when and how to draw upon the positives in my life to ease the struggle of coping day after day with life's challenges. It took practice to understand how to use my positives to be effective. It's said that practice makes perfect. I don't know if it was perfect, but it was the medicine I needed. Over time, coping became less of a struggle. When I realized I was drawing upon my positives less frequently, I knew the strength and support they provided was effective. After struggling to cope with challenges, I needed less time to heal from the side effects. Discovering additional positives to draw upon when necessary involved a continual introspective search that prepared me for future challenges. Positivity eventually grew to become an essential element of my daily life. I liked how I no longer stressed over things that in the past caused anxiety and worry. I had taken action and now was responsible and accountable to myself.

When you're feeling an emotional burden from dealing with life's challenges and situations, take a deep breath and slow down. Get away from feeling overwhelmed. Slow down and make time for your body, mind, heart, and soul to relax, regroup, and reset for positive outcomes. During this period of slowing down, draw upon your list of positives to reflect on all the good within and surrounding you. Now think with your heart to review what truly matters in your life. Make better decisions addressing your well-being.

At first, you may find it difficult and awkward to use your positives. Stay strong to continue implementing them and overcoming the stress of coping with life's challenges. The purpose of finding and using your positives is to take ownership and conquer your challenges. You can only lose if you let the challenge control you. The measuring stick of progress is when positivity continues to be more predominant in your life.

I hope you are beginning to see that finding and implementing your positives is all about your well-being. You do matter. You are important, you are appreciated, and you are the theme. Now you can begin to manage your tiring struggle of coping day after day. You can and will conquer your challenges. Follow these two steps—discovering positives and implementing them—for brighter tomorrows. Today is your fresh start to happier days.

LIFE'S NOTE 67

Three-Day Window to Serenity

For years, I found it hard to cope with life's challenges. There were times when I thought I was making progress, only to discover later I had been on a treadmill to nowhere. What I was doing wasn't helping me to cope with my struggles. After analyzing what I was doing, I discovered I was living too much in the past. I didn't want to ignore and completely forget about the past. There had to be a method to learn from the past while not dwelling on it.

> **Tip**
>
> *Learn from yesterday, celebrate today, live today to illuminate the dawn of tomorrow.*

The past was a difficult road, but I needed to again walk that journey to learn what more I needed to do to put the past in hibernation. Learning to manage and escape my feelings of pity, guilt, stress, anxiety, and confusion was paramount to overcoming my challenges. How could I begin to focus on living today, restoring and preserving my well-being and balance?

We can learn from the past and appreciate its lessons. It may be tricky, and we might prefer to bury and shield these things from our view. Using the archeologist's method of patiently digging allowed me to discover and open the chests of the past, revealing lessons for me to learn and improve. I learned that I was not responsible for the event creating this challenge. My feelings while coping with challenges were neither right nor wrong. There had to be a way to manage the stress and array of emotions.

Once I began to focus on today, I felt awareness and renewed energy. I became less negative while learning to be more positive. When I had days filled with energy, one would mirror the last with the same type of energy. Feeding on this energy, I felt increased motivation and inspiration to continue to strive to become healthier. With each passing day, things slowed down, offering more clarity and heightened awareness for clearer thought and appreciation. Learning how I lived yesterday set the stage for better living today.

Making the most of each day illuminates tomorrow for continued balance and well-being. This frees us from getting bogged down by living in the past as well as looking too far into the future. Experiences of the past, though memorable and valuable, can limit our capacity to view situations and circumstances in a new light for a fresh perspective. Trying to anticipate and predict the future, though entertaining and mystical, redirects our focus away from the moments of today that we require for happiness and fulfillment.

This method led to thinking with my heart for better decision-making and the ability to inspire myself and others. This all would have been impossible without what I call the Three-Day Window to Serenity:

1. *Yesterday*: Learn from yesterday.
2. *Today*: Live today to set the stage for tomorrow. Forecast your personal weather.
3. *Tomorrow*: What is your personal weather forecast for today? Did you learn from yesterday? Avoid looking too far into the future.

LIFE'S NOTE 68

Personal Weather

Civilizations have always had a fascination with weather and with forecasting the weather—for good reason. Today's forecasts and alerts save lives. One of television's most popular channels is the Weather Channel. Most of the time, we can either look outside or walk outside to determine the weather. However, we do not look internally to forecast and identify our personal internal weather.

> **Advice**
>
> You forecast your emotional weather. How does tomorrow look?

Your personal weather is similar to nature's weather; both have days of storms, thunder, frigid windchill, ominous clouds, and sunshine. Your emotions mimic nature's weather. The hope is your personal weather is filled with mostly warm, sunny days.

When struggling to cope with one of life's challenges, your personal weather plays a major role in your ability to cope each day. Imagine if your extended personal forecast was for seven days of rain accompanied by thunder and lightning. How would that affect your emotions and thought processes? How would you cope and make progress to manage and overcome your challenge?

The first step to improving your personal weather forecast is to look deep inside and ask, "Why are my days so emotionally dreary?" Usually you have succumbed to accepting dreary weather, and your struggle with coping has now become normal. Self-pity takes over—*why me, I cannot change, change is too much work, I'm tired*. In the word *pity* there is a *pit*, and you have fallen into it.

You can emerge from this dreary pit by stepping on the first rung of the ladder to find your positives and begin the long climb out. This will begin a path of positivity, going beyond positive thinking to brighter personal forecasts for days of sunshine and blue skies. Blustery emotions will change to warm, calm feelings of hope, satisfaction, inspiration, and happiness. Your responsibility is to paint the sky for forecasts of bright, happy days. Choose warm yellows, soft blues, and a pinch of white for healthier internal weather to help you overcome your challenges.

Use your positives to escape the lousy personal weather that has held you in a tight grip, choking your ability to cope. Once you understand that you are responsible for your personal weather and others aren't, you will be able to make the changes you seek and walk along your path basking in the sunshine of positivity.

> **Tip**
>
> *Not liking tomorrow's forecast? Live today to illuminate tomorrow's forecast.*

LIFE'S NOTE 69

Pressure Is a Red Flag

Most of us at one time or another have fallen into the trap of peer pressure. Sometime afterward, we feel disappointed in ourselves for succumbing to pressure from our peers. Peer pressure has no good outcome for the one being pressured. Those pressing us do so for a feeling of control and superiority. We are being tested for conformity and weakness.

> **Alert**
>
> *Peer pressure has no good outcome for the one being pressured.*
>
> *Walk away.*

Understanding the concept of peer pressure helps you realize the danger of giving in. A peer is someone we see as an equal. If people are applying urgent and undue pressure on us, why would we want to be their equal? Rise above and beyond to be strong and become a better person. Pressure comes when others exert urgent influence and demands on us. Those who try to influence us by force are by no means doing this with our best interest at heart. Peer pressure is ugly, selfish activity aimed only at getting control over others.

Why do we give in to the force of peer pressure? We do so to fit in, feel connected, be cool, or find a sense of belonging. We perceive fitting in as acceptance, approval, and a rise in rank or status. The perception is that those applying pressure could possibly be new friends. Just the opposite is true. They don't want friendship; they only want control. We will be labeled as weak and have lower status within the group. By giving in and conforming, we will most likely feel ostracized and treated as a subordinate or loser.

Those who are meek and weak are more susceptible to peer pressure and loss of self-esteem. The island of those saying no to peer pressure is the place for winners. Inhabitants of this island are people with high self-esteem, confidence, and the ability to think for themselves. Their dreams and hopes are preserved rather than taken away. Good outcomes and a brighter future await those saying no to such pressure.

It takes courage and will to say no to peer pressure. The opposite is saying yes from fear and weakness. You are not a lump of clay to be molded. You are important to yourself, your family, and your friends. You make a positive difference in people's lives. Staying true to self and being positive is the preferred path for less anxiety and worry. The future may not seem so bright at first. Be patient and walk away from peer pressure. Your days will become brighter and you will become a stronger person for yourself and your family. Friends will not try to influence you with peer pressure. If they do, they are not your friends and never were. Family should be your rock for trust and support. Discuss situations like this with family for a plan to protect yourself from making poor decisions. Remember, peer pressure has no good outcome for the one being pressured or those delivering such pressure.

LIFE'S NOTE 70

Bullying Must Stop Now

Bullying is nothing new. It has been around for centuries and continues to be a serious problem today. Why has bullying continued for so long? Unfortunately, some people believe that this primitive, crude behavior to control and belittle others is acceptable. Reasons for bullying go back to the primeval need for power, control, and status. These reasons continue today and can begin at home, workplaces, schools, care centers, and careers with fraternal environments. Bullying begins in early childhood and continues into old age. It must be stopped.

Alert

Bullying begins in early childhood, intensifies in school, continues in the workplace, and is present throughout life.

To conquer bullying, we must first understand it. Simply stated, bullying is tormenting another with verbal or physical attacks, including name-calling or wearing or breaking the targeted person down. Abusive peer pressure and harassment are additional methods used by bullies. Advanced techniques used to bully include the use of cyberspace and social media, e-mails, cell phones, and texting.

Why do people bully? Society in some ways encourages bullying with its emphasis on the almighty importance of winning, power, and status. We give undeserved respect to those who win and place them on a pedestal to be revered. News broadcasters and journalists focus excessive time on stories involving harm, damage, violence, crime, and negativity. This massive onslaught of reporting gives recognition and face time to bullies. The motion-picture industry does the same, drawing us to stories of darkness and danger. One of the most popular categories of books is murder mysteries. Why is it we have such a fascination with violence and spend billions of dollars to be entertained with stories of peril? Moderation in these activities could do much to cease the hurtful and dangerous behavior of bullying.

Bullies' hostility can stem from a lack of structure and accountability at home with little or no consequences. The children feel they can get away with anything. They learn early how to control others to get what they want. Additional contributing factors include early-childhood academic failures, low self-esteem, lack of inclusion, not feeling accepted, a broken home, an abusive family climate, or exposure to excessive alcohol or drug abuse. Bullying is a cry for attention. The bully cries, "Look at me," but what he or she is really saying is, "I'm insecure and I'm hurting. I need attention to get well."

An increased public national campaign of continued education coupled with a common strategy and authority by all schools, workplaces, and families toward bullying can do much to create a wave to change social attitudes to put a stop to bullying. We need to teach children, from a young age, to be compassionate and refrain from judging others, and to practice acceptance, tolerance, patience, friendship, and gratitude. Open communication at home, nurturing feelings and positive healthy behavior for sound personality and well-being.

Parents should be aware of the signs that their child is being bullied or might be a bully. Some signs are a sudden change in behavior or self-esteem, becoming aggressive, or acting unusual. Also, if a child is argumentative or disrespectful and has friends doing the same, there is need for concern. If a child is acting strange or fights and is frequently called into the principal's office, this too is a red flag requiring attention.

Parents are protective of their children, as well they should be. Fathers have a tendency to let their macho attitude blind their vision to falsely favor the perceived strength of their sons and to say, "Boys will be boys." Mothers fail to see cruelty in their daughters, saying, "She is so sweet, she would never do anything like that." Unfortunately, children can stray away from goodness to become involved in situations that are hurtful to others and themselves. Situations like bullying call for heavy-duty parenting skills to teach our children right from wrong and good from bad. It is difficult to think of or actually see our children involved in negative, hurtful behavior. Their futures are in our hands, and it is our responsibility to be grounded parents. Be aware of the signs of bullying to correct this behavior before others get hurt and, in some cases, die.

Bullies prey on those perceived as weak or different. Gays and lesbians, people with disabilities, and those society deems as being of below-average appearance are targets of bullies. If we are bullied, the natural response is to fight or argue. This response encourages bullies by giving them attention, feeding their need for power and control. Instead, believe in yourself and know that you are a good person with much to offer, and that you are loved, no matter what a bully might say. Stand tall with the courage and strength to say no or no more. Then slowly and confidently walk away to report this incident to an adult or someone in authority. If you minimize the incident or are afraid to report it, the bullying, hostility, and torment will continue.

> **Bullying Stinks**
>
> If you hurt from being bullied, don't let them control you. Believe in yourself. You do matter. Love yourself and know that others love you. Do not lose hope; do not give up.

You must take action. You did not ask for or deserve this abuse. You deserve far better. If you have experienced deep hostility and torment from bullying, seek counseling or therapy to beat the emotional trauma and become free of the grasp of the bully's influence.

To keep kids from drowning, swim instructors teach the buddy system. The same is true for dealing with or, better yet, preventing confrontations with bullies. Walk and gather in groups to prevent a possible run-in. Avoid as best you can walking or sitting alone. There is strength in numbers. Increase the numbers in your group to stop bullying.

Parents, family members, teachers, managers, caregivers, and those in authority, along with victims of bullying, must band together to teach, report, and deal with bullying to stop it before it escalates out of control, with serious results. Step forward by taking action to help those being bullied to be free of bullying's grasp. We want victims to be able to see nothing but beautiful tomorrows.

We must have the courage, either individually or collectively, to step forward and stand up to the evils of bullying. People's lives and futures are being jeopardized by ignorant, self-centered others. Victims feel too powerless, ashamed, or embarrassed to do anything or ask for help. We must be aware of the signs of bullying and take action. Bullying must be stopped and stopped now.

Signs of Bullying

- change in behavior
- change in demeanor
- wanting to be alone, quiet
- unusual argumentative behavior
- sudden use of inappropriate language
- less affection or hurtful to sibling
- anxiety, nervousness
- frequent ailments
- unexplained bruises or injuries
- substance abuse
- change in self-esteem
- loss of appetite or binge eating
- lack of sleep, frightening nightmares
- loss of possessions, such as clothing or school supplies
- unexplained requests for money
- loss of friends or unusual new friends
- not wanting to go to school or day care
- decline in academic focus and performance
- change in study habits

Tip

Include in your circle of friends only people who support you and raise your spirit.

LIFE'S NOTE 71

Moving Is a Challenge

According to the US Census, over 40 million people move each year. The majority move within the same town, county, or state. Still, millions make a long-distance move far away from familiar and comfortable surroundings. Moving near or far creates anxiety and stress. Long-distance moves far away from relatives and friends magnify the emotions of moving.

Inspiration

Rediscover and embrace family to survive the separation of relocation.

People and families decide to move for numerous reasons, including home ownership, job transfer, new job, better neighborhood, cheaper housing, shorter commute, nicer climate, and change in marital status. Do your homework and weigh the options of either moving or staying put. If possible, talk with others who made a move with similar conditions to the move you are considering. Planning and preparation are far easier than regret.

Before you decide to move, come to an agreement with your spouse on the reasons to consider moving. Share the reasons with your children to help them understand. Listen to your children's thoughts before making the final decision to move or stay put. Dealing with their feelings is extremely difficult if you are predetermined to move. Children hear that their world will be turned upside down and fear the unknown. They are scared and feel overwhelmed, with little control over or comfort in an unknown future. Talk with them to offer comfort and reassurance that everything will work out and you will always be there to listen, help, and support them. Allow at least a month or two for a period of transition to talk and prepare as a family for the finality of moving.

Once you have decided to move, talk with family, relatives, and friends about the move out of courtesy and respect, to avoid surprises and hard feelings. Communication also prepares them and you to share time together and begin to say good-byes over a period of time instead of at the last minute, with limited time to adjust.

When the day of moving has arrived, you can choose to be present at the house or go to a neutral location. Being present is difficult and mimics the process of grieving the death of a loved one. It is a difficult process, but one that is necessary to work through the steps of denial, anger, hopelessness, frustration, bitterness, and acceptance. The sight of a huge moving truck being loaded with your belongings can be traumatic and overwhelming for some family members more than others. Show patience, compassion, and tolerance, and offer expressions of comfort to help others with their feelings of loss.

Once you have moved into the new place—full of boxes to unpack, furniture to move around, beds to set up, pictures to hang, and a pantry and refrigerator to fill—take a deep breath, slow down, and work as a team to support each other. Taking time instead of rushing minimizes or ideally avoids unnecessary stress. Have tolerance for children to arrange their bedroom at their pace and to their liking. Furniture and belongings can be rearranged after allowing a period of adjustment for everyone to reach acceptance.

Know that for most families, it takes an extended period of time to adjust to and accept new surroundings and begin to make friends. Throughout this time of transition, help all family members become engaged in the new community. School activities, church, sports, volunteering, coaching, clubs, and groups all help to establish a base of connection and belonging.

Don't be shy about asking for help and suggestions to accelerate your knowledge of your new location. Include family outings to explore and discover the wealth of opportunities. Create golden moments to create new memories. Establish new routines to create familiarity and stability. We all have the need to feel comfortable in our surroundings.

Somehow, some way, a large majority of parents and children adjust and do well. Over time, new routines, new activities, new opportunities, and new memories establish a new norm of familiarity. Humans are a resilient bunch, including children. Trust that with love, all will do well.

If a family member continues to struggle with the move, seek professional help for working through this challenge, adjusting, and flourishing for today and the future. Recognizing the signs of stress sooner rather than later helps you address the emotional struggles, prevent depression, and restore balance and well-being.

Signs of Stress

- trouble concentrating
- social withdrawal—wanting to be alone
- unusual or unexpected behavior
- trouble at school
- drop in grades
- change in appetite
- change in attitude
- change in personality
- unwillingness or difficulty making new friends
- lack of motivation
- continued anger
- irritability
- frequent headaches
- difficulty sleeping
- fatigue and lethargy

> **Tip**
>
> *Become involved outside of home in your new location to emerge okay from the challenges of a family move.*

This note was written from personal experience after the challenging emotions of a long-distance move.

LIFE'S NOTE 72

Importance of Saving Money, and How to Do It

Saving money for unexpected situations and for the future is a choice. We choose to save or ignore the importance of saving. Face the music. Saving money is a must for now and the future. Giving in to peer pressure to try to live up to the Joneses has a dramatic negative impact on the pool of money available to save. The "Joneses effect" is commonly called "living beyond our means." This effect also contributes to living from paycheck to paycheck with no consideration of or discipline in saving for the future. Think logically to remove emotion from buying decisions to live within your means and save. This also lessens stress.

> **Tip**
>
> *Our means-of-living scale is usually burdened to the side of expenses. Reduce expenses to tilt the scale to favor savings.*

It is your responsibility to save for such things as security, education, unexpected expenses, and retirement. Often heard is, "We cannot save that much money," or "We do not have money to save." Review the tips below to evaluate your situation and become open to making changes.

Tips for Saving Money

- Start saving today. Procrastination costs thousands of dollars and our future.
- Start young—the younger, the better. You have a finite number of days to save for retirement.
- Have a plan. These tips will help you develop one.
- Pay yourself first. Think of this as another weekly or monthly bill.
- Save a minimum of 5 percent from each paycheck. Do your best to save more than that.

- Save to a 401(k) with the amount for the maximum company match.
- Live within your means. Instead of spending $30,000 on grown-up toys, save this amount, and over thirty years at 5 percent interest compounded annually, you'll have $129,658.27 added to your savings.
- Spend less money. Buy what you need and not always what you want.
- Shop online. Do comparisons to find the best price.
- Before buying, sleep on it to remove the emotion from the purchase decision.
- Avoid debt. Misuse of credit cards and monthly payments cost, cost, cost.
- Pay down your debt. Reduce the monthly burden and then save that money.
- Save your change. If cost is $2.01, put the 99 cents in a jar and you'll save from $150 to $600 per year.
- Compare cable TV services or eliminate cable TV in favor of online viewing.
- Shop cell-phone companies for deals.
- Climb the corporate ladder. Maximize earnings during your peak earning years.
- Develop a second income stream: online, hobby, or secondary skill.
- Take a second job, part-time—but make sure to balance with family time.

Tips for Finding Money to Save

- Make daily lunches at home and put the money you would have spent into a savings account.
- Make coffee at home or drink free coffee at work and put the money you would have spent at Starbucks or your local coffee shop into a savings account.
- Use tap water instead of bottled water and put the money you would have spent on bottles into a savings account.

- Reduce smoking by one pack a day and put the money you would have spent on those cigarettes into a savings account.
- Dine out two times less per month and put the money you would have spent at the restaurant into a savings account.
- Use online coupons when you choose the restaurant and put the money you saved on the meal into a savings account.
- Use coupons for groceries and put the money you saved at the supermarket into a savings account.
- Buy in bulk and put the money you saved over buying smaller quantities into a savings account.
- Reduce alcohol consumption by half and put the money you would have spent on booze into a savings account.

The Magic of Saving

Examples below assume a starting balance of zero dollars and interest compounded annually. The annual yearly amount saved is the starting balance beginning the second year and assuming the same amount is saved each year for twenty-nine years.

- Save $535 per month to save $6,420 per year for twenty-nine years with 5 percent interest to save $426,537.40.
- Save $390 per month to save $4,680 per year for twenty-nine years with 5 percent interest to save $310,933.81.
- Save $190 per month to save $2,280 per year for twenty-nine years with 5 percent interest to save $151,480.57.

Saving money reduces anxiety and stress. It brightens your future now and at retirement age. Imagine retiring with little or no savings. Procrastinating to save compounds and continues the struggle. Start now and save, save, save.

[These are the views of the author and there is no claim of financial expertise. The views are based on simple common-sense practices. The compound-interest calculator used can be found at http://bit.ly/dWWXh.]

Your Notes

What challenges are you facing and how will you overcome these challenges?

What are your positives and how will you implement them to manage and overcome your challenges?

Do you allow either Mother Nature or others to forecast or influence your personal weather? If so, why?

Conclusion
Keep the Faith

The decade of the 1960s popularized the phrase "keep the faith." It was kind of like the verbal extension of the peace sign. It is our guess as to its meaning in this situation. Some definitions might be faith to achieve world peace, to beat the establishment, to hang in there. Your guess is as good as mine.

Sports organizations commonly use "keep the faith" as a slogan to motivate the team and fans through the period of a slump. "Keep the faith" is much more than a phrase to encourage the outcome of athletic competition. Our well-being can be served by this phrase to help us all through times of struggle.

Faith in our gifts and abilities, along with self-esteem, can help us surpass our self-defined limitations. Imagine the alternative of not believing in yourself and its ramifications on your quality of life. Belief in yourself gives you self-worth and the confidence to be strong when things get tough. You refuse to give in or give up. You keep the faith.

Follow the path of goodness to discover the power of divine faith. Your attempts to stay the course will be challenged by skeptics and doubters to test your commitment to your faith. Collectively, they will attempt to crack your will. Believe, and you will be blessed.

Spirituality is a light and a reminder to live a life of goodness and moral excellence. When you question your faith, meditate or pray for strength to search deeper for meaning and purpose. A life of meaning and purpose is built on faith. Lay a solid foundation for faith to last and endure through all.

Some may say faith is belief from the mind or heart. Faith seems to be much more, and it goes beyond man's earthly comprehension. Divine faith seems to reside in the soul. Each of us has the ability to awaken this faith. Do we have the will?

A life of goodness is a way to nurture our well-being and awaken our will to have the faith to believe. No matter the attempts by others to question our faith or our coping with challenges, struggles, and tribulations, keep on believing, stay the course, and remain free from self-doubt. Your belief and faith will snuff the questioning of others and ease the pain of coping with your struggles. You will endure.

Nurturing and preserving your well-being promotes openness to learning and considering ways to be a better person. Self-improvement is a ceaseless journey as we strive for meaningful purpose to share goodness with others. Life is more about sharing our gifts than about ourselves. Goodness is keeping the faith.

About the Author

Steve attributes his heightened consciousness to his life experiences and challenges faced over sixty-one years. He counts his blessings—from his loving, supportive parents and sister to his wife of thirty-eight years, Julie, and their three remarkable, loving children. Two grandsons are the icing on the cake, as well as two of Steve's go-to positives.

Diagnosis and treatment of cancer in 2011 motivated him to write *Finding Your Positives* to share his story of a plan to face the struggle of coping with life's toughest challenges. The following year brought the scare of a heart attack. This was a defining moment, further heightening his consciousness to write about the elements of a life of abundant goodness.

The idea to share wisdom on topics affecting life's decisions surfaced as a way to share a guide of notes for his children and grandchildren to reference. Thus *Life's Notes: Down-to-Earth Insights for Well-Being* was born. The hope is that its numerous notes remind or enlighten others to live a life of happiness and abundant goodness.

In addition to writing books, Steve does motivational speaking before groups of people who are coping with difficult challenges. He has been a guest on numerous radio shows from New York City to Los Angeles. Books Without Borders chose *Finding Your Positives* as one of the books featured for the month of December 2012.

Alphabetical Listing of Notes

CPSIA information can be obtained at www.ICGtesting.com
Printed in the USA
BVOW07s1751291213

340340BV00001B/58/P